AMERICA'S TOP WW II

ACES

IN THEIR OWN WORDS

EIGHTH AIR FORCE

AMERICA'S TOP WW II

ACES

IN THEIR OWN WORDS

EIGHTH AIR FORCE

WILLIAM HESS

MBI Publishing Company

First published in 2001 by MBI Publishing Company, Galtier Plaza, Suite 200, 380 Jackson Street, St. Paul, MN 55101-3885 USA

MBI Publishing Company books are also available at discounts in bulk quantity for industrial or sales-promotional use. For details write to Special Sales Manager at Motorbooks International Wholesalers & Distributors, Galtier Plaza, Suite 200, 380 Jackson Street, St. Paul, MN 55101-3885 USA

On the front cover: Capt. Robert S. Johnson claimed 27 aerial victories over enemy fighter aircraft in World War II. *USAAF*

On the back cover: Maj. Don S. Gentile piloted a Spitfire, a P-47D, and a P-51D during the war, scoring 21.83 victories. *USAAF*

Library of Congress Cataloging-in-Publication Data Available

ISBN 0-7603-1338-5

Edited by Peter Bodensteiner
Designed by Stephanie Michaud

Printed in USA

CONTENTS

INTRODUCTION

The combat reports contained in this book are copies of the actual reports filed by the top Eighth Air Force aces in World War II. On return from their combat missions, all pilots were interrogated and instructed to report any enemy aircraft destroyed, probably destroyed, or damaged in the air. Likewise, pilots reported aircraft destroyed or damaged on the ground as well as damage to tanks, vehicles, armored equipment, and all types of enemy installations and equipment. As the reader will note, some of the pilots' reports convey a great amount of detail of their actions while others describe actions briefly. Some reports are terse, some are lengthy, and some even contain a bit of humor.

I gathered many of these reports from the official unit histories, which are on deposit at the U.S. Air Force Historical Archives at Maxwell Air Force Base in Alabama. However, the bulk of my collections come from the priceless microfilm work done by my very good friend, Dr. Frank Olynyk, during research

U've had it!, Capt. John England's aircraft in invasion stripes. Note the rearview mirror above the windshield. *Olmsted*

for his *Credits For Destruction Of Enemy Aircraft* studies. Frank found the vast majority of the pilots' combat reports for the Eighth Fighter Command on deposit at the National Archives in Suitland, Maryland.

I have included selected reports from each ace who had an air-to-air score of 14 victories or more, plus two others: Robin Olds and Chuck Yeager. Samples of Olds' and Yeager's reports are included at the editor's request in view of their presence in more recent history. Unfortunately, we cannot include all of these aces' combat reports in this volume. Doing so would entail reproducing about 350 reports.

I hope that the reader will enjoy reading these reports and the short biographies and photos of the men and their aircraft that I have put together.

—*William N. Hess*

THE FIGHT FOR
AIR SUPERIORITY

Portrait of a fighter pilot just back from a long combat mission.
Capt. Richard Peterson's face shows what flying on oxygen, constant
maneuvering, and sitting on an iron seat can do to a pilot. *Olmsted*

When the Eighth Air Force inaugurated the heavy bom-
bardment of Europe in August 1942, Maj. Gen. Ira Eaker
felt that his bombers would be able to take care of themselves.
There would be no need for fighter escort. The primary job of the
Eighth Fighter Command would be fighter sweeps over the Continent and support of the bombers as they went across the English
Channel and on their return from their missions. The first few
heavy bomber missions by the Boeing B-17s were intercepted by

the Luftwaffe, who looked them over but did not press attacks.

It was not long, however, before the enemy began to make passes at the Flying Fortresses. In doing so, the Germans found that the four-engine craft had its weak spots, primary among them a lack of armament in the nose. The Luftwaffe could make line-abreast attacks from 12 o'clock, and it would result in bombers falling to their guns just about every time.

This did not alarm the bomber advocates. The bombers' claims for enemy fighters destroyed were enormous and field modifications for additional armament for the nose of the B-17 were initiated immediately.

It didn't take long, though, before Eaker and his staff realized that the bomber claims against the Luftwaffe fighters were grossly overstated. Had they been true, the Luftwaffe would have been drastically short of fighters.

The fledgling Eighth Fighter Command was called to work. In the spring of 1943 the fighter strength of the Eighth Fighter

Capt. Walter Beckham and his ground crew. When he was drowned while strafing on February 22, 1944, Beckham was the top ace of the Eighth Air Force, with 18 aerial kills. *USAASF*

Command consisted of the Fourth Fighter Group, made up of the old Eagle Squadrons; the 78th Fighter Group, which had come to England with long-range P-38s but had been stripped of them to support the 12th Air Force in North Africa; and the 56th Fighter Group, which had just arrived from the United States with its Republic P-47s. Before things could really get under way, all three groups had to be equipped with the P-47.

The Spitfire pilots of the Fourth Group had a fit upon learning that they would have to give up their sleek little fighters for Thunderbolts. The 78th Group was having to rebuild with replacement pilots, and while its command types were unhappy not to get new P-38s, they went to work to make the best of what they had. The 56th had received the first Thunderbolts available from the factory, trained on them, and loved them.

Miss Fire was Capt. Fred Christensen's final aircraft. Although some kid Christensen about his six Ju 52s in one day, all the rest of his kills were fighters. *USAAF*

Col. Hubert "Hub" Zemke, CO of the 56th Fighter Group. He trained and took the first P-47 Thunderbolt group to England. There they became famous and accounted for the highest number of aerial victories— 664.5—in the Eighth Air Force. *USAAF*

In May 1943 the fighters began their missions to aid the bombers. The range of the P-47 was only about 175 miles, which was just enough to get them across the English Channel. Col. Hubert Zemke, commander of the 56th Group, began his crusade to the Eighth Fighter Command for two primary items. He wanted auxiliary fuel tanks desperately, and he also wanted paddle-blade propellers, which would give the Thunderbolt a better rate of climb. Regretfully, he got very little action in regard to the fuel tanks, and Maj. Gen. Frank O'D. Hunter, didn't seem to be interested. It would be August before a very inefficient and unstable 200-gallon tank was carried by the group for the first time. During the summer, 75-gallon, and later 108-gallon, tanks appeared, which would become mainstays with the Thunderbolt group.

Even though the P-47s had been limited to restricted action, they had engaged the Luftwaffe on numerous occasions and been successful. The Eighth Air Force got its first ace on July 30, 1943, when Capt. Charles London of the 78th Fighter Group scored his fifth victory.

New units also arrived in England. Three more P-47 groups arrived in July—the 352nd, the 353rd, and the 355th. Limited Thunderbolt range was still a big problem, however. All the fighters could do was escort to the limit of their endurance and then turn the bombers over to the Luftwaffe. Sixty bomber losses on the Schweinfurt-Regensburg missions of August 17, 1943, did not sit well with Gen. H. H. Arnold, commander of the U. S. Army Air Forces. Further group reinforcements arrived during the month, but these did not help the problem.

The change that did help was when Maj. Gen. William E. Kepner took over from Major General Hunter. Kepner completely changed the fighter tactics of the command and put them on the offensive. Fighters were no longer required to stay so close to the bomber stream. They were now asked to check enemy aircraft whenever they appeared in the vicinity.

The Eighth Bomber Command took tremendous losses in October 1943, which included a further 60-plane loss on the repeat mission to Schweinfurt on October 14. The Eighth Air Force took a long look at its status and decided that its fighter escort missions would have to play a much greater part in its operations if the strategic air offensive was to be maintained. Fortunately, things were looking much better in the Eighth Fighter Command. Two P-38 units, the 20th and 55th Fighter Groups, had arrived, bringing the capability of long-range escort. Two more P-47 units, the 356th and the 359th Fighter Groups, had arrived to add numbers to the Thunderbolt force. The P-47s now had access to 108-gallon drop tanks, which gave them a range of 340 miles. With the new fighter strength, it was possible for the fighters to work in relay teams, dividing escort duties to penetration escort, target escort, and withdrawal escort. This gave the bombers full-range coverage that improved their protection immensely.

The fall of 1943 brought the escort aircraft the Eighth Air Force yearned for: the North American P-51 Mustang long-range fighter. It didn't originally arrive for the use of the Eighth Air Force, however. It was assigned to the Ninth Air Force and designated for tactical use after the invasion of the continent.

Col. Donald Blakeslee, in his cockpit, made sure that his Fourth Fighter Group became one of the first to get the P-51 Mustang. *USAAF*

When the officers of the Eighth Fighter Command found out what the P-51 could do, though, they knew they had to have it. The aircraft had a 475-mile range without drop tanks! The 354th Fighter Group, which was equipped with the new plane in England, was immediately attached to the Eighth Fighter Command for escort duties. The Eighth Air Force would get its own Mustang group in January 1944, when the 357th Fighter Group arrived. Not to be outdone, Lt. Col. Donald Blakeslee of the

Fourth Fighter Group insisted that his group had to have P-51s, and he got them in February 1944.

Capt. Gerald Johnson became one of the first aces in the 56th Fighter Group. He would score 15.5 victories with the unit and one with the 356th Fighter Group before he fell to flak and became a prisoner of war. *USAAF*

January 1944 brought about a monumental change in the Eighth Air Force. Maj. Gen. James Doolittle took over command from Maj. Gen. Ira Eaker. By this time it was known that the invasion of the European continent would take place by the summer of 1944. It was essential that air supremacy be achieved over the Luftwaffe before the invasion. On the first visit made by Doolittle to the Eighth Fighter Command, it is said that he saw a sign on the wall that read, "The mission of Eighth Fighter Command is to protect the bombers." Doolittle ordered the sign taken down and replaced with one that read, "The mission of Eighth Fighter Command is to destroy the Luftwaffe."

A major step was taken toward this end during what would become known as "Big Week." The entire week beginning on February 20, 1944, was set up for the heavy bombers to strike at aircraft and engine manufacturers. These missions were supported by strikes on similar targets by the 151st Air Force, flying from Italy. While the destruction of the factories bombed on these missions might not have been as great as hoped for, the Luftwaffe suffered irreplaceable losses. During this week alone, the Eighth Fighter Command claimed 287 aerial victories against the loss of 85 of its own.

March 1944 brought about the duty that many aircrew members had been waiting for: a raid on Berlin, the capital of the Third Reich.

The mission was scheduled for March 4, but weather prevented most of the force from arriving over the target. The big day came on March 6. More than 700 Eighth Air Force bombers attacked targets in the capital city, losing 60 of their number against hordes of German fighters. The escort fighters claimed 81 victories for the day against only 11 losses.

The bombers went back to Berlin on March 8, with 320 bombers attacking targets in the city. Once more the Luftwaffe

Here are three top guns of the 4th Fighter Group. Left to right: Capt. Duane Beeson, Maj. Don Gentile, and Maj. James Goodson. Who would have the luck in this kind of card game? *USAAF*

was very prominent. Thirty-seven bombers were lost, but once more the fighters were triumphant, as 77 German fighters fell to their guns.

On March 9, when some 339 Eighth Air Force B-17s deposited their loads on the German capital, eight bombers fell to flak. The Luftwaffe was not present! Their absence was proof that the U.S. Army Air Force had gained superiority over the German Air Force.

Petie 2nd, Lt. Col. John Meyer's aircraft, ready for a mission, carrying drop tanks. *USAAF*

The Long Reach and Tactical Air

Although the Luftwaffe was no longer capable of opposing the heavy bombers on all of their missions, it did exert significant force on occasion. However, new fighter groups and the continuing conversion to P-51 Mustangs gave the Eighth Fighter Command a force that was capable of escorting the bombers to targets anywhere in Germany.

As Allied ground forces were taking part in their final preparations for the invasion of the Continent, it was imperative that the heavy bombers begin to strike at tactical targets in France. All transportation facilities had to be knocked out; bridges, railroad installations, trains, and motor transport had to be attacked.

When D-Day arrived on June 6, 1944, all fighter forces flew multiple missions. The most surprising development of the day was that the invasion forces were completely free of any attack by the Luftwaffe! As the Allied ground forces began to move inland, fighters of the Eighth Fighter Command, the Ninth Air Force, and the Royal Air Force completely covered the skies. Ground forces moved swiftly once they broke out of the Cherbourg Peninsula, and it seemed as though the war in Europe might be over by the end of 1944. Unfortunately, the Germans were able to pull enough men back into the homeland to make a very determined stand.

The Eighth Fighter Command was once more primarily committed to escorting the bombers to strategic targets. Operations with the bombers seemed to do quite well and losses were drastically reduced. Yet, on days when a rendezvous was missed or a bomber group got out of the bomber stream while the Luftwaffe was up in force, the bombers could suffer drastically.

A new weapon introduced by the Luftwaffe was the heavily armored Focke-Wulf 190A-R8, which carried a pair of 30-millimeter guns along with its machine guns and 20-millimeter weapons. These fighters could make short work of the bombers, if they could get to them. The Eighth Fighter Command pilots loved to catch these "Destroyer" units, because the weight of their armor cut their maneuverability to the point that they became relatively easy targets.

As the fall of 1944 neared, the Eighth Air Force turned its attention to a very important strategic target—oil. From that time until the end of the war in Europe, oil refineries became the most important targets in Germany. These refineries also became the most heavily defended installations in the Third Reich, and they were spots where the Eighth Fighter Command pilots could always look forward to opposition from the Luftwaffe.

Complete Supremacy

From October 1, 1944, until the end of the war in Europe, Allied aircraft enjoyed complete supremacy in the skies over Germany. That is not to say that there were no Allied losses. Intense flak and limited interception by the Luftwaffe indeed cost all Allied forces a certain number of aircraft. There were a few instances where American bombers strayed from the bomber stream and suffered accordingly.

The skies over Germany had become so dominated by Allied fighters, and the fuel shortage was so bad, that the Luftwaffe found it almost impossible to train new pilots. Many of Germany's novice pilots found themselves flying with the veteran fighter groups after only 50 to 60 hours of flying time. Many new Me 109s and long-nose FW190Ds were lost in crashes by the young pilots just trying to fly from one location to another. These novices would be led against the bombers by one or two veteran pilots, who told them to ignore the escorting fighters and continue on to the bomber stream. In such cases, some Luftwaffe pilots continued to fly straight and level to their destruction. Others bailed out as soon as Allied fighters positioned themselves on their tails.

The actual demise of the Luftwaffe took place on January 1, 1945, when all available German fighters took off on "Operation Bodlenplatt." This was a low-level mission to destroy Allied aircraft on bases primarily in Holland and Belgium. This mission turned out to be a real fiasco. Two hundred thirty-two fighters were lost to enemy action, while more than 50 fell to accidents and flak. Two hundred fourteen pilots were lost, with 151 killed and an-

Capt. Raymond Wetmore's aircraft, all painted down in invasion stripes. It looks more like the censor painted the aircraft serial number out. *359th Fighter Group Association*

other 63 taken prisoner. Around 150 Allied aircraft were destroyed. After suffering these losses, the Luftwaffe never again possessed the strength to attack en masse.

The highlights, as they were, for the Luftwaffe in the spring of 1945 included the operation of the jet-powered Me 262 and the rocket-driven Me 163. If the Me 262 had been in production for fighter usage earlier with an improved engine, it certainly would have been a menace to the American bombers. The operations of the Me 262 were greatly handicapped by the presence of myriad Allied fighters. Their bases had to be protected by Focke-Wulf 190Ds, but the Focke-Wulfs were being savaged by the Mustangs. One hundred thirty four German jets were officially credited to the Eighth Fighter Command pilots.

Aerial action continued until the end of hostilities in Europe. The final Eighth Air Force fighter victory was scored on April 25, 1945, before hostilities ceased on May 8, 1945.

Capt. Leonard "Kit" Carson

THE
ACES

The combat reports contained in this book are those of the top scoring hunters of the Eighth Air Force. The tenacity of these men put them in the forefront of their units and made them leaders of groups, squadrons, flights, and elements. All were good pilots, most were very good shots, all were blessed with excellent eyesight, and all were determined to engage the enemy whenever possible, regardless of the odds. All except a couple believed in teamwork and discipline in confronting the enemy. Two of these aces, much to the chagrin of their group leaders, were hard to keep in formation and had a tendency to be lone eagles. Luck held out for one of them.

These aces proved themselves in numerous ways. Only one of them was ever downed in air-to-air combat, and that was the work of a lucky aerial gunner, not an enemy fighter pilot. Several of these men, however, fell to enemy ground fire while at the peaks of their careers.

When one considers that only a small percentage of the thousands of fighter pilots would turn out to be hunters, it makes the deeds of this elite group stand out even more. It must also be considered, however, that there were other hunters who simply did not find the enemy often enough in their quests. Regardless of the circumstances, these top scorers in this book were fortunate enough to find the action they desired. These men certainly proved their mettle through their accomplishments.

✪Maj. Clarence E. Anderson Jr.

16.25 Victories

Capt. C. E. "Bud" Anderson rests on the wing of *Old Crow,* his personal Mustang. Anderson scored 16.25 victories with the 363rd Fighter Squadron of the 357th Fighter Group. *USAAF*

Clarence E. Anderson Jr. was born on January 13, 1922, in Oakland, California.

He entered the U. S. Army Air Force Aviation cadet program and graduated from flight training at Luke Field, Arizona, on September 29, 1942. He was subsequently assigned to the 363rd Fighter Squadron of the 357th Fighter Group. Anderson went overseas with the group in November 1943 and entered combat in February 1944, flying P-51 Mustangs. Anderson was a very successful fighter pilot and flew two combat tours with the 357th Group; 12.25 of his victories were scored on his first combat tour.

Anderson remained in the Air Force following the war and commanded fighter units in both Korea and Vietnam. He retired from the Air Force as a colonel on March 31, 1972.

As a civilian he worked for McDonnell–Douglas Aircraft Corporation as manager of its flight test facility at Edwards Air Force Base, California.

Anderson presently lives in retirement in Auburn, California.

Decorations: Distinguished Flying Cross with 4 Oak Leaf Clusters, and Air Medal with 13 Oak Leaf Clusters.

Assigned aircraft in World War II:

P-51B 43-24823 B6-S, *Old Crow*

P-51D 44-14450 B6-S, *Old Crow*

```
TYPE OF MISSION:Combat
DATE:30 April 1944
UNIT:363rd Fighter Squadron
357th Fighter Group
TIME:1145 hours
LOCATION OF ACTION:30 miles southeast of Orleans
WEATHER:Hazy
TYPE OF ENEMY ENCOUNTERED:FW 190
CLAIM:One FW 190 destroyed
```

I was leading Cement White following Red Section, and we had left our bombers about 10 minutes earlier and were proceeding home. We approached a box of bombers and I saw enemy fighters buzzing around them. I called Red Section and we went over full throttle. Six FW 190s came through my section head-on. Two broke down and the others turned right. By using 20 degrees of flaps and a full throttle, I pulled around on their tails in one turn and started firing. It must have scared the hell out of them, as they hit the deck. I then picked out two together and followed, attacking the first man and getting three good bursts. He was smoking badly and pieces flew off. I then had to pull up as I was overrunning him. He straightened out and ran.

I then rolled back and followed. As I closed again, a blue-nosed P-51 came in very steep and fast in front of me. He pulled up and out, the FW 190 pulled up, and the pilot bailed out. The ship crashed and I don't know whether the blue nose ever fired. He was coming in so fast and at such an angle that I don't think he could have hit him if he did fire. I claim one FW 190 destroyed.

–Capt. Clarence E. Anderson Jr.

```
TYPE OF MISSION: Combat
DATE: 8 May 1944
UNIT: 363rd Fighter Squadron, 357th Fighter Group
TIME: 1205 hours
LOCATION OF ACTION: Solltau, Germany
WEATHER: 10/10 at 6,000 feet
TYPE OF ENEMY AIRCRAFT ENCOUNTERED: FW 190
CLAIM: One FW 190 destroyed
```

I was leading Cement Squadron, which consisted of nine ships, on an escort mission to Berlin. We had left the bombers about 10 minutes earlier when we saw 20-plus bandits heading toward the bombers. We chased, even though we were low on gas and numbers. They could have outrun us if they had gone on straight, but they circled tightly to the left, staying in close formation. We zoomed up above them and turned with them about five times, as the last ships in the formation split-essed for cloud cover. We were at about 24,000 feet and the clouds were at about 6,000. When about half of the FW 190s had broken off for the clouds, the leader rocked his wings violently and they all scattered, making for the clouds below. We all then jumped in. Picking one out, I closed to fair range and fired several bursts. We were in a left-circling dive. I got very few hits but did see some on the right wing and a big flash in the tail section. The FW 190, after being hit, rolled over into a much steeper dive. I followed for a while but control became difficult. I noticed the airspeed was close to 600 miles per hour. This was at about 8,000 feet, so I let him go and pulled out as gently as possible. Lieutenant Pierce, my number three, had followed one below the clouds and was coming back up when he saw two P-51s break off an FW 190. The FW 190 continued on the dive, his tail breaking off and catching fire before going in the clouds. I did not see this happen myself, as I was too busy trying to get out of my own dive. Capt. W. A. Rogers, a flight leader in the same encounter, lost his entire wing following one of the FW 190s as they broke up. I later saw the combat film and realize it is not too impresive as to hits, but I fired several bursts and with no over-run control on my ship at the time, the effect of the last part of the burst is not known.

Capt. C. E. Anderson's P-51B, in which he scored his early victories. Note the invasion stripes and 104-gallon drop tanks. *Olmsted*

I believe I weakened the FW 190 enough to cause his tail to come off at the terrific rate at which we were diving. The way Lieutenant Pierce described the two P-51s breaking off, and considering the fact that Lieutenant Pierce and myself were the only ones with any claims in this encounter, I'm sure, although I did not see it myself, that the FW 190 I fired upon was destroyed. I claim one FW 190 destroyed.

Ammunition expended: 740 rounds

–Capt. Clarence E. Anderson Jr.

```
TYPE OF MISSION:Combat
DATE:27 May 1944
UNIT:363rd Fighter Squadron.
TIME:1230-1245 hours
LOCATION OF ACTION:North and west of Strasbourg
WEATHER:Light haze
TYPE OF ENEMY AIRCRAFT ENCOUNTERED:Me 109
CLAIM—Two Me 109s destroyed
```

I was leading Cement White section, and our squadron had just joined the bombers when combat was heard over the Radio Transmission in the front boxes. We started that way when my number three called in four bandits coming in on us from four o'clock. We broke into them and they pulled up and circled, trying to get at us. With full throttle and rpm at 28,000 feet, I was able to close around and climb on them. They all straightened out and tried to run level while their number four climbed up. My number three, Lieutenant Simpson, climbed up after him while I chased the other three. They tried to outclimb us, then they tried to outrun us level but could not. I closed slowly on number three, waited until I was close and dead astern, and then fired a good burst, getting hits all over. Pieces flew off, smoke streamed, and his canopy may have come off. He rolled over and went smoking down out of control. I could not watch him as the other two were right in front of me. I singled out number two. He dove and pulled up in a left climbing turn. I pulled inside and overshot. He straightened out and I pulled up to 100 miles an hour watching him as he tried to get on my number-two's tail. He stalled out and I went after him. He repeated with another left climbing turn. I overshot again, and the same thing followed. The third time I made up my mind I wouldn't lose him, so as he pulled up for the third time I fired. I was in prop wash, going almost straight up in a left climbing turn. The first tracers went

This is the final *Old Crow*, which Capt. C. E. Anderson flew during his second tour with the 357th Group. He scored an additional four victories during this period.

over his right wing. I skidded my nose over and strikes appeared all over—an explosion occurred. I slid alongside and saw fire break out. It rolled over slowly and went straight in and crashed from 26,000 feet. Lieutenant Skrha, my wingman, was with me and saw the whole encounter. I claim two Me 109s destroyed.

Ammunition expended: 529 rounds .50-caliber MG

—Capt. Clarence E. Anderson Jr.

✪Maj. Walter C. Beckham

18 Victories

Capt. Walter C. Beckham of the 351st Fighter Squadron, 353rd Fighter Group, was only about 5 feet 6 inches tall and 135 pounds, but he could rack his Thunderbolt with the best of them. *USAAF*

Walter Carl Beckham was born on May 12, 1916, in Paxton, Florida.

Beckham joined the U.S. Army Air Corps in April 1941 as a flying cadet and received his wings and commission on December 12, 1941. His first assignment was to the Panama Canal Zone. On his return, he was assigned to the 353rd Fighter Group, with which he was sent to England, flying P-47 Thunderbolts. Beckham became a very successful pilot in the P-47. At the time he was shot down strafing on February 22, 1944, his 18 victories had made him the top ace of the Eighth Air Force.

Following his release from a German prison camp, he was promoted to lieutenant colonel.

Beckham remained in the Air Force after the war, earned a Ph.D. in physics, and became a nuclear weapons scientist. He remained active in this field until his retirement as colonel in 1969.

Beckham continued his career as a nuclear scientist in civilian life until he retired in Albuquerque, New Mexico. He passed away in Albuquerque on May 31, 1996.

Decorations: Distinguished Service Cross, Silver Star with 3 Oak Leaf Clusters, Distinguished Flying Cross with 4 Oak Leaf Clusters, and Air Medal with 5 Oak Leaf Clusters.

Assigned aircraft in WW II:

P-47D 42-8476 YJ-X, *Little Demon*

```
TYPE OF MISSION:Combat
DATE:3 February 1944
UNIT:363rd Fighter Squadron
TIME:1100 hours
LOCATION OF ACTION:Vicinity of Oldenburg
WEATHER:Not Stated
TYPE OF ENEMY AIRCRAFT ENCOUNTERED:Me 109
and FW 190
CLAIM:One Me 109 destroyed and one FW 190 destroyed
```

I was leading Roughman White flight, flying with about 10 of the 350th Squadron planes. Twelve-plus Me 109s, at least 1,000 feet above us, came from our three o'clock as we were flying northward. Even with their altitude advantage, they made no attempt to attack us, but tried only to escape. We turned into them, swinging around in about a 270-degree turn to the right, and gave chase.

In this case, the P-47 definitely outclimbed (29,000 to 32,000) the 109, outturned, and outdived it. As we climbed and closed, the 109s to the rear began half-rolling by ones and twos. P-47s gave chase. I waited until the lead planes dived and followed one down in an almost vertical dive. I cut throttle to avoid compressibility, but stayed about the same distance from the

From the scoreboard on the fuselage, this was made in early October 1943, just before he hit his stride. Before the end of the year, Capt. Walter Beckham would have 11 victories. *USAAF*

109. I opened throttle and closed, fired, and got hits and pieces. I followed this with more strikes, and I don't believe the pilot was able to get out. I pulled out and saw the 109 continue straight down into a cloud layer at 7,000 feet at a speed in excess of 400 miles per hour.

I used my high speed to zoom back up to 15,000 feet. At this altitude, between two cloud layers, seven FW 190s passed in front of me at right angles to my line of flight. They were in good formation with a flight of three leading and a flight of four slightly behind and to the right. I turned right, closed easily, and fired from astern on the one on the extreme right. I got strikes and pieces, including the canopy. Flame from the engine extended along the left side of the fuselage and the plane spun. The two flights of three each flew serenely along as I nosed down into the clouds and set course for home at about 6,500 feet.

The apparent lack of awareness on the part of other enemy pilots leads me to believe that with more ammunition, I might have moved up and destroyed several others. My guns had not stopped firing, but I had fired a burst or so after the tracers appeared that indicate there are only 50 rounds in each of the four guns. My electric sight was insecurely fastened, making for inaccurate shooting and wasteful ammunition expenditure. I found it necessary to move the stick back and forth as I fired, thus throwing away a lot of bullets. The gun-sight trouble is now corrected.

—*Maj. Walter C. Beckham*

```
TYPE OF MISSION: Combat
DATE: 8 February 1944
UNIT: 351st Fighter Squadron
TIME: 1212 hours and 1225 hours
LOCATION OF ACTION: St. Hubert vicinity
WEATHER: Not Stated
TYPE OF ENEMY AIRCRAFT ENCOUNTERED: Me 109
and FW 190
CLAIM: One Me 109 destroyed and one FW 190 destroyed
```

As we rendezvoused with the leading two wings of bombers at 1210 hours, I saw two Me 190s flying parallel with us, about 1,000 to 1,500 feet above. We used full power, climbing up and catching them. We went from about 26,000 to 29,000 feet in this climb. I fired several bursts. One Me 109 flipped over and dove almost straight down, using definite evasive maneuvers on the way. I stayed about the same distance behind with the throttle nearly closed and was unable to get any good shots going down. I pulled out with difficulty. Three other members of my flight saw a pilot bail out of one of the 109s. Colonel Rimerman and several others saw one of them crash into the ground.

We regained 25,000 feet of altitude and rejoined the bombers. Twenty-plus FW 190s were observed at three o'clock to the bombers. I chased two of them beneath a cloud in a left turn, picking the one on the inside of the turn. The one on the right pulled up and dived down in what I thought to be an attempt to get on my tail. Because of this, I fired long bursts at about two right deflection and excessive range in an attempt to finish the job quickly and get into the clouds. I was agreeably surprised to see strikes and continued firing as I closed. The FW 190 rolled onto its back at about 1,000 feet of altitude and dove. As I pulled up and to the right, I saw him crash into the ground, making a large mass of flames. I don't know if the other FW 190 tried to attack me or not.

On the way home, through a break in the clouds, I saw an airfield with 8 or 10 planes parked. I was able to line up three or four of them in a dive out of the sun from about 6,000 feet at about 400 miles per hour indicated. I got a lot of strikes on and in front of a twin engine. I encountered no return fire, although a flak tower was just northeast of the field.

I was disappointed to see as I passed over these planes that they were dummies. They were models of He 111s, Me 110s, and at least one Me 109. I believe it almost impossible that we will ever see such tempting targets sitting close together, without camouflage, that are not Nazi tricks. I recommend that we confine our attacks on planes on the ground to those more definitely identifiable as the real McCoy.

–*Maj. Walter C. Beckham*

✪Maj. Duane W. Beeson
17.3 Victories

Capt. Duane Beeson and *Boise Bee,* his Thunderbolt, in which he downed 11 enemy aircraft. *USAAF*

Duane W. Beeson was born on July 16, 1921, in Boise, Idaho. Beeson went to Canada early in the war to join the Royal Canadian Air Force. He completed flight training in Canada on February 26, 1941, and was sent to England in March 1942. He had just reported to No. 71 Eagle Squadron when the unit was transferred to the U.S. Army Air Corps. Beeson became a pilot in the 334th Fighter Squadron of the Fourth Fighter Group. While most of the former Eagle Squadron pilots were bemoaning their fate in the P-47 Thunderbolt, Beeson really took to the aircraft. He became one of the first aces in the plane and would score 12 victories in it.

Beeson was downed by flak while strafing a German airfield on April 5, 1944, and became a prisoner of war.

Promoted to lieutenant colonel after his return from POW camp, Beeson stayed in the Army Air Force. Unfortunately, he would succumb to a brain tumor on February 13, 1947, in Washington, D. C.

Decorations: Distinguished Service Cross, Silver Star, Distinguished Flying Cross with 6 Oak Leaf Clusters, Air Medal with 3 Oak Leaf Clusters, and Purple Heart.

Assigned aircraft in World War II:
P-47D 42-7890 QP-B, *Boise Bee*
P-51B 43-6819 QP-B, *Boise Bee*

```
TYPE OF MISSION:Combat
DATE:29 January 1944
UNIT:334th Squadron
TIME:1110 hours
LOCATION OF ACTION:Vicinity of Aachen
WEATHER:10/10 at 3000 feet about 500 feet
thick-100 miles visibility above
TYPE OF ENEMY AIRCRAFT ENCOUNTERED:Me 109
and FW 190
CLAIM:One Me 109 destroyed and one FW 190 detroyed
```

We sighted approximately 15 Me 109s and FW 190s flying near the bombers, and when Pectin squadron attacked them they went into a dive. As our squadron bounced this group of enemy aircraft, I saw about 6 other Me 109s coming in to get on the squadron's tail. Lieutenant Chatterly and I turned into these.

Capt. Duane Beeson assesses damage to the tail of his aircraft. Soon the odds would catch up with him, and he would be downed by flak on April 3, 1944. At that time, Beeson was probably the top ace in action with the Eighth Air Force. *USAAF*

One of them put a hole in my tail-plane before we could turn onto them, but when the turn was completed I saw Lieutenant Chatterly on the tail of a 109, shooting and getting very good strikes. These 109s also started to dive. I got on the tail of the nearest one and opened fire at 250 yards, closing to about 50 yards. I was using API ammunition and saw very severe strikes on the fuselage and wing roots, then a large flash somewhere in the cockpit area. The enemy aircraft flicked violently to the right and went down, trailing a long stream of gray-black smoke. This combat took place from 23,000 feet down to about 15,000 feet, and the last I saw of the 109 he was going down through 10/10 cloud below.

I was then alone and saw a combat going on far below, so I started down again when I sighted an aircraft off to starboard also diving. When I went over to investigate, he turned out to be a yellow-tailed FS 190 with a belly tank. I don't think he saw me as I was approaching him out of the sun, but he steepened his dive a little and I was closing on him slowly, so I fired a burst out of range trying to slow him down. No results were seen so I continued behind him as he went into cloud at about 3,000 feet. When he came out below, I was about 300 yards behind. I opened fire again and saw many incendiary strikes on the fuselage. He dropped his nose at about 200 feet altitude and went into the deck. I then pulled up in a zoom to 5,000 feet, where there were many P-47s of Greenbelt Squadron, and I came home with them. I claim one Me 109 and one FW 190 destroyed.

—1st Lt. D. W. Beeson

```
TYPE OF MISSION: Combat
DATE: 25 January 1944
UNIT: 334th Fighter Squadron
TIME: 1245 hours
LOCATION OF ACTION: Beckingen
WEATHER: Clear
TYPE OF ENEMY AIRCRAFT ENCOUNTERED: FW 190
CLAIM: One FW 190 destroyed
```

I was flying in Pectin Green One position as our group was giving cover along the bomber track. As we approached the leading box from the rear, Captain Care reported something at three o'clock to us, and I sighted two fighters at our same level (25,000 feet). Then as we turned in their direction I saw a lone Fortress, which had fallen far out to the right and below his formation. Two other fighters were making passes at it, so we opened up and dived toward them. Before we could reach them, the Fortress slowly fell off to the starboard and began to spiral down while the two fighters circled around as though to come in again. When they saw us coming after them, one dived away and the other whipped into a turn, giving about a 60-degree shot. I fired and missed. Then, as we had nearly 500 miles per hour indicated, I was able to zoom up above him and come down again for another attack. This time he dived for the deck, giving me a chance to come in on his tail. He was taking evasive action all the way down, which made it hard to get a good shot. Then he circled around a small town and leveled out along a small stream, so I opened fire at about 300 yards and closed to 100 yards before breaking away. There were good strikes along his fuselage, and his starboard wheel dropped down. As I overshot him, he dropped off and headed toward the ground. I lost sight of him at this point as we were reforming our section, but Lieutenant Monroe says he saw the FW 190 strike the ground. As we started to climb we saw eight or nine parachutes very near, which had probably come from the Fort.

–Capt. D. W. Beeson

```
TYPE OF MISSION: Combat
DATE: 1 April 1944
UNIT: 334th Fighter Squadron
TIME: 1044 hours
LOCATION OF ACTION: North of Lake Constance
WEATHER: 7/10 Cumulus at 8,000 feet
TYPE OF ENEMY AIRCRAFT ENCOUNTERED: Me 109
CLAIM: One Me 109 destroyed
```

I was leading Pectin Squadron as we escorted several boxes of Liberators in the vicinity of Lake Constance. The bombers had just turned north when I sighted four aircraft making a pass at a box of bombers that were quite far away. They were coming line astern to the bombers from ahead and below. When I first saw them, we opened up and went after them, but as we were so far away it took a while to close. A single Liberator had fallen out of formation and was smoking very heavily; many chutes came out of it and it went into a steep climb. These four aircraft climbed after the Lib, and as we came closer we could recognize them as Me 109s.

I picked the last one and began to close, but then as I just came into range, another Mustang flew above him and he broke for the deck so I had to chase him down. After following him after a couple of flick rolls, I got on him again and opened fire at about 200 yards, closing to 100 yards, and saw quite severe flashes and heavy smoke coming out. I broke off at about 7,000-feet altitude, where the enemy aircraft exploded as it hit the ground. I claim one Me 109 destroyed.

—Capt. D. W. Beeson

```
TYPE OF MISSION:Combat
DATE:8 October 1943
UNIT:334th Fighter Squadron
TIME:1455-1510 hours
LOCATION OF ACTION:Meppel-Zwolle vicinity
WEATHER:High cirrus, Visibility good.
TYPE OF ENEMY AIRCRAFT ENCOUNTERED:Me 109
CLAIM:Two Me 109s destroyed, and one Me 109 damaged
```

I was flying as Green leader in Pectin Squadron. As we were coming up into position behind the bombers, we sighted 30 or more Me 109s above us trying to get into the sun to attack the squadron. The squadron turned, trying to throw them. Then I sighted two Me 109s coming in behind Blue section and called for the section break. I turned violently and got on the tail of this enemy aircraft and fired about 200 rounds, height 23,000, seeing strikes around the port wing root, then flames and smoke came out of his engine.

He slowly turned over, his prop windmilling, so I broke off and took a good look around.

At this time I saw a parachute at about the place where Blue Three was hit and Lieutenant Fraser, my number-two man, also saw another chute below, which he thinks came from my Me 109. Then two more Me 109s came down from above and I fired a burst at one of them, 45 degrees head-on, seeing a few strikes on his port wing. Lieutenant Fraser fired at the other one. As our section started to come out at about 19,000 feet, a lone Me 109 stooged by in front with his finger well up. I closed to about 150 yards and shot him down, observing him strike the ground. I claim two Me 109s destroyed and one Me 109 damaged.

—1st Lt. D. W. Beeson

✪Col. Donald J. M. Blakeslee
14.5 Victories

Former RCAF fighter pilot Donald J. M. Blakeslee would become one of the top fighter leaders in the Eighth Air Force and CO of the Fourth Fighter Group. *USAAF*

Donald James Matthew Blakeslee was born September on 11, 1917, in Fairport Harbor, Ohio.

Blakeslee joined the U. S. Army Reserve in 1938 as a second lieutenant in the infantry. He was honorably discharged in 1940 in order to join the Royal Canadian Air Force. He arrived in England as a pilot in March 1941. Blakeslee flew a number of combat missions with No. 401 Squadron in Spitfires. During this time he destroyed one enemy aircraft and damaged several others. He later joined No. 133 Eagle Squadron as a flight leader. With this squadron he was credited with another two victories.

When the Eagle Squadrons transferred to the Fourth Fighter Group in September 1942, Blakeslee transferred as a captain in the 335th Fighter Squadron. Shortly thereafter he was promoted to major and given command of the squadron.

His leadership qualities were swiftly realized, and he became group operations officer and was promoted to lieutenant colonel in July 1943. He served in this position until he took command of the Fourth Fighter Group in January 1944, when he was promoted to colonel.

Blakeslee was able to get his group equipped with P-51 Mustangs in February 1944, and his unit excelled in its operations after the change. Blakeslee continued to be one of the very top fighter unit commanders in the Eighth Air Force, and his efforts as a tactician and disciplinarian paid great dividends.

Blakeslee also commanded the 27th Fighter Escort Group in Korea during 1950 and 1951.

He retired from the Air Force in April 1965.

Decorations: Distinguished Service Cross with Oak Leaf Cluster, Silver Star with Oak Leaf Cluster, Distinguished Flying Cross with 6 Oak Leaf Clusters, Air Medal with 5 Oak Leaf Clusters, and the British Distinguished Flying Cross. For his service in Korea he was awarded the Legion of Merit, a sixth Cluster to the Distinguished Flying Cross and 4 additional Clusters to the Air Medal.

Assigned aircraft in World War II:
Spitfire 5b BL 776
Spitfire 5b BL 545
P-47 D 42-7863 WD-C
P-51B 43-6437 WD-C
P-51B 42-106726
P-51D 44-134779 WD-C

```
TYPE  OF  MISSION:Combat
DATE:29 May 1944
UNIT:Head Quaters, Fourth Group (with 336th Squadron
TIME:1350 hours
LOCATION  OF  ACTION:North of Falkenburg and
Dievonow Seaplane base
WEATHER:Clear
TYPE  OF  ENEMY  AIRCRAFT  ENCOUNTERED:Me  410
and Do 18
CLAIM:One Me 410 destroyed, and two Do 18s damaged
```

I was leading the group on an escort of bombers to Posen. As we were flying to the port of the lead box of bombers at 1350 hours, two aircraft were reported at nine o'clock and 2,000 or 3,000 feet below us, climbing up to bomber level from seven o'-clock. I identified them as Me 410s, and I turned hard starboard with two sections, dropped tanks, and opened up.

The Me 410s made a pass at the second box of bombers, getting strikes on several Forts, then going on through the formation from zero to four o'clock. They split-essed and went into a diving turn, one breaking to the right, the other to the left. We all went after the one that broke right. My number two, Lieutenant Netting, and Lieutenant Emerson from the second section got within range before I did and they chased it down. I followed them and was watching for it to crash when I saw the other Me 410 at 1,000 feet to port and west of where the first one crashed. He dove straight to the deck and I followed line astern, opening fire at 200 yards, closing to 100, and overshot him. I saw strikes all over his tail, cockpit, wings, and engine. I broke above him and to the left. I saw him crash into the woods and set them afire.

After this engagement we returned and climbed to the north. When at 6,000 feet, a seaplane base identified as Dievonow was reported and we saw it underneath us. We made a diving port turn to the deck, came up to it from south to north, making one pass at 14 Do 18s anchored on the lake. We came in by sections, four abreast, each pilot choosing a separate target. I saw strikes all over my first one. On my second one I saw strikes on the engine with smoke resulting. I did not see it burn or sink. I claim one Me 410 destroyed and two Do 18s damaged.

–*Col. Donald J. M. Blakeslee*

```
TYPE OF MISSION:Combat
DATE:2 July 1944
UNIT:Fourth Group, with 336th Squadron
TIME:1045 hours
LOCATION OF ACTION:Over Budapest
WEATHER:Low Clouds
TYPE OF ENEMY AIRCRAFT ENCOUNTERED:Me 109
CLAIM:One Me 109 destroyed
```

I was leading the group on a bomber escort mission to Budapest from base in Italy. We arrived in the target area 15 minutes prior to bomber time and conducted a sweep at 25,000 feet. No enemy aircraft were seen, so I led 336th Squadron down to attack an airdrome southwest of Budapest, leaving the other two squadrons up for cover.

When we had dropped down to 18,000 feet, Captain Hively of the 334th Squadron reported 40 to 50 smoke trails coming in from the north at 27,000 to 28,000 feet. Captain Hively turned north to intercept and I led my squadron northeast in a climb in order to cover the bomber track over the target. We were 1,000 feet below and to the south when Captain Hively attacked the lead enemy aircraft as they started a diving attack against the bombers. Several sections of the 336th Squadron attacked the enemy aircraft as they came down through the formation from the attack above.

I arrived at 27,000 feet with six aircraft to join the melee of

P-51 was the mount for Col. Donald Blakeslee in many of his 14.5 victories. Blakeslee never liked the idea of putting personal markings on his aircraft. USAAF

fighters. I dove to attack an Me 109 that had started to attack a lone bomber, but he passed underneath me and I lost sight of him. I ended up from this attack at 17,000 to 18,000 feet northeast of Budapest, alone, with 12 Me 109s above me coming in from the southwest. They were apparently diving away from the general engagement, and when they sighted me they started to attack.

There was a thin layer of haze just above me, and I took advantage of this for cover. We all circled a few times, and as I was getting ready to fire at the last enemy aircraft, the first one was getting on my tail. I nipped back up to the base to break away, made a 180-degree turn, and then came back down to find the enemy aircraft still circling and in position. I repeated this maneuver three times, but the enemy aircraft were still there. The fourth time they were gone, and I sighted a lone Me 109 flying just under the haze layer.

I attacked from astern, same level, and gave a two-second burst from 150 yards.

The pilot bailed out. I returned to the general melee and joined up several sections of four P-51s. I claim one Me 109 destroyed.

–Col. Donald. J. M. Blakeslee

✪Maj. Leonard K. Carson
18.5 Victories

Capt. Leonard "Kit" Carson, early in his combat career. Carson downed five enemy aircraft and became an ace on his first tour, but really went to town on the second. *Olmsted*

Leonard Kyle "Kit" Carson was born in 1923 in Falls City, Nebraska.

Carson entered the U.S. Army Air Force in April 1942 as an aviation cadet and graduated from flight training on April 12, 1943. He joined the 362nd Fighter Squadron of the 357th Fighter Group in January 1944. He flew two tours of combat with this unit and became one of the top scoring aces still in Europe at the end of the war.

Carson remained in the Air Force following the war and became involved in aerodynamic experimentation and flight testing.

He retired from the Air Force as a colonel in April 1968, and following his retirement worked in the aerospace industry.

Carson passed away on March 8, 1994.

Decorations: Silver Star with Oak Leaf Cluster, Distinguished Flying Cross with 2 Oak Leaf Clusters, Air Medal with 16 Oak Leaf Clusters, and British Distinguished Flying Cross.

Assigned aircraft in World War II:

P-51B 43-6634 G4 C, *Nooky Booky*

P-51D 44-13316 G4-C, *Nooky Booky II*

P-51D 44-14896 G4-C, *Nooky Booky III*

P-51D 44-11622 G4-C, *Nooky Booky IV*

```
TYPE OF MISSION:Combat
DATE:27 November 1944
UNIT:362nd Fighter Squadron, 357th Fighter Group
TIME:1300 B.S.T.
LOCATION OF ACTION:South of Magdeburg
WEATHER:CAVU
TYPE OF ENEMY AIRCRAFT ENCOUNTERED:FW 190
CLAIM:Five FW 190s in the air. Three pilots bailed
out; two did not.
```

I was leading Blue Flight of Dollar Squadron, providing escort for another fighter group. We were in the vicinity of Magdeburg, Germany, when two large formations of bandits were reported. One of the formations, still unidentified, made a turn and came toward us at eight o'clock. We dropped our tanks and turned to meet them. We tacked on to the rear of the formation, which consisted of 50-plus FW 190s. I closed to about 300 yards on the nearest one and fired a medium burst with no lead, getting numerous strikes. He started to burn and went into a turning dive to the left. I believe the pilot was killed. He never recovered, but crashed into the ground and exploded.

I returned to the main formation, again closing to the nearest one at the rear. I opened fire at about 300 yards, firing two short bursts, getting strikes all over the fuselage. He started to smoke and burn. He dropped out of the formation and turned to the right until he was in a sort of a half split-ess position, never recovering from this attitude. I saw him crash and burn. The pilot did not get out.

Closing again on the main formation, I pulled in to the nearest man, at about 400 yards. I fired a short burst, noting a few hits. He broke violently to the left and I broke with him. I picked up a lead on him and fired two more bursts, getting strikes on the cockpit and engine. He started to smoke and burn badly. The pilot jettisoned the canopy and bailed out. I watched him fall for quite a distance but did not see his chute open. The FW 190 crashed about 50 yards from a house situated in a small town.

I could still see the main formation about a mile ahead of me. While starting to catch them, I saw a straggler on the deck. I dropped down to engage him but he saw me coming. He turned left away from me and I gave chase for about three minutes before I caught him. I opened fire at about 400 yards, getting strikes on the right side of his fuselage. He turned sharply to the right and I picked up a few degrees lead, firing two more bursts, getting more strikes on the fuselage. The pilot jettisoned his canopy and bailed out. As I was chasing this one, another formation of 40 FW 190s passed about 500 feet above and 400 yards in front of me. They made no attempt to engage me or to help their fellow Jerry. They continued on a heading of 20 to 30 degrees.

I pulled up after my last engagement and set course for home base when another FW 190 came in at my wingman and me from seven o'clock high. We broke into him and he started a zooming climb. I chased him, gaining slowly. Suddenly he dropped his nose and headed for the deck. I gave chase and caught him in four or five minutes. I opened fire at 400–450 yards, but missed. I closed further and fired another burst, getting several strikes on the fuselage. The plane started to smoke. I fired again as he made a slight turn to the right, observing more hits on the fuselage. Then the pilot jettisoned his canopy and I broke off my attack to the right. I waited for him to bail out but he didn't, so I turned to engage him again. I was still about 700 yards away when the pilot pulled the nose up sharply and left the ship. His chute opened a couple seconds later.

During the entire encounter, my wingman, Flying Officer Ridley, remained with me. I do not believe his performance as a wingman could be surpassed. I claim five FW 190s destroyed in the air.

Ammunition: 1,620 rounds expended

–Capt. Leonard K. Carson

```
TYPE:OF MISSION–Combat
DATE:2 December 1944
UNIT:362nd Fighter Squadron, 357th Fighter Group
TIME:1320 B.S.T.
LOCATION OF ACTION:Vicinity of Bingen, Germany
WEATHER:Cirrus at 30,000; stratus at 18,000; low
broken at 6,000
TYPE OF ENEMY AIRCRAFT ENCOUNTERED:Me 109
CLAIM:Two Me 109s destroyed, two pilots killed
```

I was leading Dollar Squadron on a bomber escort mission when the bombers made a 180-degree turn about five minutes from the target. Microwave Early Warning control reported the enemy airborne 15 miles south of target. We continued in this area at 18,000 feet and were approaching the Rhine River at Bingen when 15–20 Me 109s initiated an attack at five o'clock. We dropped our tanks and turned into them. I singled out a flight of three and followed them into a thick haze. They dropped beneath the haze and I closed on tail-end Charlie, firing a burst at 350 yards, getting strikes on the fuselage. I closed a bit further and fired another burst, getting more strikes on the fuselage. Pieces came off his ship and it started to smoke. He went into a tight spiral to the right and crashed. The pilot did not get out.

I turned to attack the remaining two 109s. They split and I followed what I thought was the leader as he dived for the deck. I closed to about 400 yards and fired a burst, getting no hits. I closed further and fired a long burst, getting strikes all along the left wing and fuselage. He started to smoke and burn. He was about 20 feet above the water of the river. He pulled up and headed for a field on the other side. He made the field but did nearly a half roll at about 100 feet and went into the ground. Again, the pilot did not get out. I claim two Me 109s destroyed in the air.

Ammunition: 600 rounds expended

–Capt. Leonard K. Carson

```
TYPE OF MISSION: Combat
DATE: 14 January 1944
UNIT: 362nd Fighter Squadron, 357th Fighter Group
TIME: 1240 B.S.T.
LOCATION OF ACTION: 20 miles northwest of Berlin
WEATHER: CAVU
TYPE OF ENEMY AIRCRAFT ENCOUNTERED: FW 190,
Me 109
CLAIM: Two FW 190s, One ME 109 destroyed
```

I was leading Blue Flight of Dollar Squadron while giving escort to the first, second, and third boxes of bombers. We were sitting on top of the lead box, about 1,000 feet above, when two very large gaggles of enemy aircraft were spotted at 12 and 11 o'clock coming head-on. They were immediately identified as

FW 190s with top cover. We pulled out in front of the bombers and met them in a head–on attack. I took Blue, Green, and Yellow Flights to the left to break up the attack at 11 o'clock. I fired at them head-on, as did most everyone else, and then turned and tacked on to the rear of the gaggle. Their attack on the bombers had been diverted so we concentrated on the tail-end Charlies. I closed to about 400 yards on an FW 190 at the rear of the outside, firing a good burst and getting strikes all over the fuselage. I watched him for a second to see his reaction. He took no evasive action but just peeled off to the right very slowly. I followed him down. His turns became more violent and then he started snapping from the right to the left. He was smoking quite badly. I believe the pilot was killed. I pulled off and watched him until he hit the dirt.

I went back up to the bombers and looked around for a couple of minutes. I looked straight back at six o'clock and saw a formation of 40 to 50 FW 190s coming up about 1,000 yards behind. There were a couple of P-51s near me and they broke with me. We met the enemy airplanes head-on. They didn't fire, but we did, although I saw no hits. After we got behind them, we turned as quickly as possible and once again picked out a tail-end Charlie. I fired a burst at 350–400 yards at an FW 190, getting strikes. He did a couple of snaps to the right with his belly tank on, and wound up on his back. I fired again, getting more hits on the fuselage. Pieces came off the enemy ship and he began smoking. He split-essed and headed for the deck. I followed him down until he hit, bounced, and crashed. The pilot did not get out.

I climbed back up to about 4,000 feet, and two Me 109s came tooling by abut 2,000 feet beneath me. I dropped down and fired at the one in the rear, getting no hits. They dropped flaps and broke violently. I pulled back up while they circled in a Lufbery. I made another ill-timed pass and pulled up again,

This is *Nookie Bookie IV*, in which Capt. Leonard Carson scored a number of his victories late in the war. *Olmsted*

getting no hits. The leader broke off and headed for the deck. I dropped down on tail-end Charlie as he started down. He pulled up, losing speed. I kept my excessive speed, fire-walled it and started firing at about 300 yards. Closing down to about 200 yards, I got hits all over the fuselage. His coolant blew as I pulled over him. Then he went into a sort of tumbling spiral and crashed. I claim two FW 190s and one Me 109 destroyed.

Ammunition: 1,050 rounds expended

—Capt. Leonard K. Carson

✪Capt. Frederick J. Christensen Jr.
21.5 Victories

Capt. Fred Christensen peeks over the edge of the cockpit with his lucky black cat. Christensen set great credence on the appearance of the cat. *USAAF*

Frederick Joseph Christensen Jr. was born on October 17, 1921, in Watertown, Massachusetts.

Christensen had attended Boston University and MIT before he entered the U.S. Army Air Corps. He graduated from pilot training on December 7, 1942, at Napier Field, Alabama. In August 1943 he joined the 62nd Fighter Squadron of the 56th Fighter Group in England. In the course of 107 combat missions with the group he scored 21.5 victories and reached the rank of captain.

Christensen left the Air Force at the end of the war and became active in the Massachusetts Air National Guard, where he reached the rank of colonel.

Decorations: Silver Star, Distinguished Flying Cross with 6 Oak Leaf Clusters, and Air Medal with 2 Oak Leaf Clusters.

Assigned aircraft in World War II:

P-47D 42-75207 LM-C, *Rozzie Geth*

P-47D 44-26628 LM-C, *Miss Fire/Rozzie Geth*

```
TYPE OF MISSION:Combat
DATE:15 April 1944
UNIT:62nd Fighter Squadron
TIME:Approx. 1430 hours
LOCATION OF ACTION:Altona
WEATHER:Hazy
TYPE OF ENEMY AIRCRAFT ENCOUNTERED:Me 109
and FW 190
CLAIM:One Me 109 and one FW 190 Destroyed
```

I was leading Groundhog Squadron. The three squadrons of the group had just split to pick up their representative ground-strafing targets. I flew down to the outskirts of Hamburg, losing altitude all the while. I crossed the river to Altona airdrome. Here there were many enemy aircraft on the ground. I then gave the order to drop tanks. Groundhog White Three called in bogies at nine o'clock and we went down to investigate. With the sun on our tails, I began to bounce. They were flying at 5,000 feet, six tight abreast with one straggler off the left flank and another off the right flank. I dove under the one on the left, pulled up and positively identified it as a clipped-wing Me 109. I noted no braces under the elevators. I started to fire at 350 yards and continued firing to 200 yards. The enemy aircraft was covered with hits. The majority of hits were concentrated from the engine back to the underside of the cockpit. The 109 seemed to stop in midair and I saw an internal explosion just forward of the cockpit. It went into a turn to the right and fell straight down, burning profusely and shedding large pieces.

I then attacked an FW 190 with a deflection shot. I noticed a few strikes and turned him in a 270-degree turn. He then straightened out, and as I chased him I saw the Me 109 I had previously fired at crash on the ground to my left. I threw on water injection and closed quite rapidly on this FW 190, which was hugging the ground and just missed the trees in front of him. I kept firing short bursts at him, observing a few hits each time. I saw many hits on one of my last bursts. In the meantime, an FW 190 was on my tail, but too far behind to do any damage. Still firing at the 190 in front of me, I observed black smoke pouring from his fuselage. Finally the enemy aircraft hit a tree with his left wing, spun around, and cartwheeled through the trees.

The 190 behind me was getting quite dangerous so I broke into him. He tried to follow me and we made one orbit together, pulling streamliners the whole time. I used the remainder of my ammunition, threw on water injection, and began to climb in tight spirals. The enemy aircraft gave up at 4,000 feet, for I was outturning him and outclimbing him. I then headed west, picked up my wingman and headed home. The Jerrys seemed very aggressive and very experienced. I claim one Me 109 destroyed and one FW 190 destroyed.

—Capt. Fred J. Christensen Jr.

```
TYPE OF MISSION: Combat
DATE: 7 July 1944
UNIT: 62nd Fighter Squadron
TIME: Approx. 1045 hours
LOCATION OF ACTION: Vicinity Gardelegen
WEATHER: Clear, visibility excellent
TYPE OF ENEMY AIRCRAFT ENCOUNTERED: Ju 52
CLAIM: Six Ju 52s destroyed
```

I was leading Platform Squadron on July 7. We had rendezvoused with the bombers and escorted them longer than we were scheduled. I passed over Gardelegen airdrome and noted much activity on the field. Upon closer observation I saw aircraft landing. I continued on course, dropping my altitude from 17,000 and made a large, 360-degree orbit. I watched very closely and picked up about 12 aircraft, which I later identified as Ju 52s. They were flying toward the field in pairs and in st form. I ordered my flight to attack. I forgot to drop my wing tanks, but this helped cut my speed for the attack. I saw them peeling off to the left and making a huge orbit down the field. I entered the traffic pattern from above, went by the last Ju 52, and shot at the next one in front of me. I observed strikes on his wings and left engine, but passed over him before I could see any further results. My wingman said it burned and exploded in midair after I passed over him.

I then lined up the second and shot from quite close range, registering hits on both wings and fuselage, causing huge flames to bellow back. The third Ju 52 was in a turn to the left. I fired a 15-degree deflection shot, noticing many strikes. The right gas tanks were on fire when I ceased firing. He tried to land in a field short of the airdrome, but the flames increased and the aircraft burned on the pasture.

On the next attack, on another Ju 52, my engine quit and I spent precious moments switching gas tanks. I went by him and dropped my tanks at the same time. I then found myself above another Ju 52. I took a short squirt at this enemy aircraft and noticed a few hits. He then tried some evasive action by putting his tail in the air in a 60-degree angle. Because he was only approximately 100 feet off the ground, he couldn't pull out and crashed.

I then lined up dead astern on the fifth and waited until I was very close before firing. The hits were concentrated around the wings. Both wings were burning as I went by, and the enemy aircraft peeled off to the right and dove into the ground.

Capt. Fred Christensen of the 62nd Fighter Squadron, 56th Fighter Group, in the cockpit of *Rozzie Geth,* named for his girlfriend. Christensen would score 21.5 victories with the 56th. *USAAF*

The last one was right in front of the fifth enemy aircraft, just off the edge of the field. I pressed my attack through the flak and gave him a good burst in both wings. Flames were coming back from the outer tanks but he tried to land anyway. He did and burned in the middle of the field. In the meantime I had to do a 180-degree turn to evade the fierce flak. I retraced my original path, hugging the ground the whole way. I counted 9 fires, including the one on the field. The 10th had crashed in the town where I couldn't see him.

There were three Me 109s on the field and 25-plus Ju 52s and U/I aircraft. The 52s were black and difficult to see against the forest. The flak was really intense. I claim six Ju 52s destroyed.

—Capt. Fred J. Christensen Jr.

✪Col. Glenn E. Duncan
19.5 Victories

Col. Glen E. Duncan was CO of the 353rd Fighter Group and was credited with 19.5 victories before he went down strafing. Behind him is a P-51 named Dove of Peace. He spent from July 1944 until nearly the end of the war in Europe with the Dutch underground. *USAAF*

Glenn Emile Duncan was born on May 19, 1918, in Bering, Texas.

Duncan entered the Army Air Corps in February 1940 and graduated from flight school at Kelly Field, Texas, on October 4, 1940. Duncan had considerable fighter experience and was a major when he joined the 353rd Fighter Group in 1943. The group entered combat in August 1943 flying P-47 Thunderbolts. He was a very successful fighter pilot from the beginning and became one of the higher-scoring aces in the organization. In November 1943, he assumed command of the group and was promoted to lieutenant colonel. When he was downed by flak on July 7, 1944, he was a colonel. Duncan was never captured. He joined the Dutch underground and operated with them until April 1945.

Following the war Duncan served as commander of several fighter wings and saw service with NORAD. He retired from the Air Force in February 1970.

Decorations: Distinguished Service Cross, Silver Star, Distinguished Flying Cross with 7 Oak Leaf Clusters, and the Air Medal with 3 Oak Leaf Clusters.

Assigned aircraft in World War II:

P-47D 42-8634 LH-X, *Dove of Peace IV*

P-47D 42-7988 LH-X, *Dove of Peace*

P-47D 42-25506, *Dove of Peace VI*

P-47D 42-25971 LH-X

```
TYPE OF MISSION:Combat
DATE:24 January 1944
UNIT:350th Fighter Squadron
TIME:Approx. 1240 hours
LOCATION OF ACTION:Vicinity of Tirlemont
WEATHER:8/10 to 10/10 patchy cirrostratus, base
19,000 feet. Visibility 3 to 4 miles
TYPE OF ENEMY AIRCRAFT ENCOUNTERED:Me 110
CLAIM:Two Me 110s Destroyed
```

We were on area support for heavy bombers in area near Ans, Germany. I was leading the group, flying with Pipeful Squadron. We had been patrolling our designated area, with the lead squadron at 22,000 feet; the second squadron, Roughman, as high cover at 33,000; and the third squadron, Wakeford, at 25,000 acting as a bouncing squadron. At 1215, recall was given and I began a slow descent in order to fly under a layer of cirrus. Lead was in good combat formation and under a thick layer of cirrus. Wakeford Squadron was to my right at about 16,000 feet. Roughman Squadron was above the cloud at about 26,000 feet.

I was just getting the R.A. at having flown another milk run mission when I saw two airplanes off to my left and low. They were easily recognized as two-engines, and as we closed they were definitely identified as Me 110s. By this time I was down under a layer of cumulus at 7,000 feet and could see four Me 110s in line formation, flying at 5,000 feet on a heading of 230 degrees. I had full throttle, turbo back to slow. I made a sharp left turn, then swung to come in behind the last Me 110. Still, I was closing too fast so I threw in a few good-hearted skids and then at the last moment, having overshot and messed up a good shot, barrel rolled on the Hun's tail. I closed up to about 200 yards, centered the needle and ball, put the pip on top of the cockpit, and squeezed off a good, long burst.

The Me 110 immediately began losing extra parts and flamed up. (They burn nicely.) I must have killed the rear gunner in the first few rounds because he was not shooting. This Me 110 veered off to the left and down and then crashed. During this time the other Me 110s had made a sweeping turn to the right and were now in line-astern formation. Incidentally, three were black and one was white.

I pulled over the Me 110 that I had just shot down and came in behind the number three or next-in-line. This rear gunner was really excited and shooting like mad. They must be very poor gunners, because I held my fire until I pulled up to about 250 or 300 yards and then gave him a good long squeeze. (I found out later that I picked up one .303 slug in the right side of my engine from this gunner.) He immediately burst into flames and pieces flew everywhere. These eight-fifties pack a wallop. This Me 110 went into a sharp spiral and crashed into a woods, causing the entire area to be enveloped in a blazing inferno. Neither the pilot nor the gunner was able to get out of the ship. I saw the gunner burning nicely as he tried to get out but couldn't, and the pilot wasn't fast enough before the ship crashed.

By this time I was up on the white Me 110, which had gone down to tree-top level and was heading toward the Vaterland.

The Me 110s didn't know which way to turn as two flights of P–47s were in there by now and would not let go. I chased the white 110 and saw strikes on the rear and right wing tip, but this was my last few rounds of ammunition. I was firing with empty guns for about 10 seconds before I finally realized that it was not my poor shooting but because my guns were empty. I cursed a few seconds for someone to come get the bastard. I had no sooner pulled away from behind the Me, when Capt. Newhart opened fire and the Me 110 crashed in a woods.

By this time all the Me 110s had been shot down and the various P-47s had gathered together as much as possible and headed home. As I turned to go home I had two more P-47s with me, Captain Newhart and Lieutenant Zoiner. They knew that I was out of ammunition so one flew on one side and line abreast. We pulled up to about 5,000 feet heading 318 degrees so that I could get a recognizable landmark and I saw that we were southeast of Brussels.

About this time we came on a nice airdrome near Tirlemont, Belgium, when we saw an enemy aircraft landing. Gosh, I thought, what I wouldn't give for a bit of ammunition and another tank of gas. Captain Newhart, seeing an Me 109 landing, went down and shot him up. I will confirm a destroyed for him. It was nice shooting. At the same time Captain Newhart went down, I saw three FW 190s circling to the west of the drome at about 2,000 feet. As Lieutenant Zoiner and I turned, I called Lieutenant Zoiner and Captain Newhart to come on and we would be getting out. I watched in the mirror for possible pursuit of the FWs and finally saw one chasing Newhart. I called for full throttle and a dive to deck. The FW was firing explosive ammunition but he was out of range and they were bursting about 300 yards to the rear of Newhart. It is interesting to note that we three were pulling "balls out" and indicating about 350 miles per hour and easily outdistanced the FW. As soon as I thought that we had lost him completely, I called for Zoiner and Newhart to pull down to 2,000 revs and 35 inches of mercury. We went along this way for about five minutes and were just beginning to pass over a town, when the FW caught up with us and began shooting. I took immediate violent evasive action. Lieutenant Zoiner, being on my left, turned into the FW and shot. The FW turned to the left and Lieutenant Zoiner came out on his tail. He managed to damage the FW, and then came on with Newhart and me. By this time the gas problem was getting touchy. All that combat and chasing was no help in the conservation of gas.

We were now pulling 30 inches of mercury and 1,400 rpm and below the trees. In fact, Lieutenant Zoiner took the side branches of one tree without much damage to the ship. This low flying was a breach of flying regulations, and we were also tied down by orders not to shoot a thing in occupied territory, even the flak tower. So, our low flying was our only defense against the flak that was kicking up dust all around us. We went across the center of Brussels, Ghent, and Osteland, as turning away from

This is the original personal insignia on Col. Glen Duncan's P-47. He called it *Angel of Death*, Higher authority did not like it, so he changed his insignia to *Dove of Peace*. USAAF

our course to go around the towns meant using more gas. We finally came out of enemy territory at Osteland, and they do have lots of very good flak gunners. They even shot heavy stuff at us. It looked like a ship going into the water every time one of them hit. Well, we evaded the stuff successfully and took up a heading to Manston.

I received a very good and efficient homing from Bluefrock and came into Manston after three hours and forty-five minutes in the air. Newhart and Zoiner were with me. I claim two Me 110s as destroyed and confirm one Me 110 and one Me 109 for Captain Newhart.

–Lt. Col. Glenn E. Duncan

```
TYPE OF MISSION: Combat
DATE: 6 March 1944
UNIT: 352nd Fighter Squadron
TIME: Approx. 1200 hours. First encounter
approx. 19,000 feet, second encounter down
to 3,000 feet
LOCATION OF ACTION: Vicinity of Steinhuder Lake
WEATHER: 5/10 overcast at 6,000 feet
TYPE OF ENEMY AIRCRAFT ENCOUNTERED: FW 190
CLAIM: 2 FW 190s destroyed
```

I was leading the group, consisting of eight sections, making two squadrons of 16 P-47s each. We made rendezvous with the Third Division B-17s and left a section of eight ships to give escort to the rear box. As the rest of the group was closing up the middle box, some 12-plus FW 190s made a head-on pass through the Fort formation northwest of Steinhuder Lake. If we could have been one minute earlier we could have stopped the attack, but due to the time element we were only able to engage the enemy aircraft as they came out of the rear of the bomber formation. Two Forts were seen shot down by the pass, which was not any fair trade for the four enemy aircraft that I saw go down immediately after the attack.

I went down with both wing tanks on, dropping one as I closed on the FW 190. I was able to close, but not fast enough, so I shot some long-range bursts, hoping to be lucky for once in my life. I reckon my shooting is not too good yet. I'll study some more charts now.

After a few seconds of chasing, I closed to about 500 yards and caused the FW to roll over. He was sucker bait then. I stayed with him through thick and thin. (The wing tank was still pushing gas into the good ol' engine.) Finally, after patient and incessant firing, I managed to get enough strikes in the wings and cockpit to kill him. He went down. By this time the wing tank was dry, so I dropped it and had to run and help my number two, who had an FW on his —-; I mean his tail. Lieutenant Geurtz was having a lot of fun outdiving the Jerry, but we weren't doing any good that way so I cut in and chased him away. I was unable to kill him as the bombers were still getting attacked and we pulled back up to them. There were many P-47s in the area, causing some confusion, but we managed to recognize them at the moment before shooting.

I saw one FW 190 northeast of Steinhuder Lake starting to go after the bombers, so I tacked onto his tail. I chased him around through a few gyrations and finally managed to hit him going in a heavy dive indicating about 550. He splattered nicely in a German town. I claim two FW 190s destroyed, two pilots destroyed, and one German house blown up by their own fighter.

–Lt. Col. Glenn E. Duncan

```
TYPE OF MISSION:Combat
DATE:12 June 1944
UNIT:351st Fighter Squadron
TIME:0629 to 0653
LOCATION OF ACTION:Vicinity of Evreux and Dreux
airdromes
WEATHER:Layer 8-9/10 cumulus, base 3,000, top
4-5000 feet
TYPE OF ENEMY AIRCRAFT ENCOUNTERED:Me 109
CLAIM:Three Me 109s destroyed
```

I was leading the group with Lawyer Squadron. We were on a bomb-and-strafing mission against enemy lines of communications and had arrived at our area near Evreux. We let down through cloud cover and began looking for targets. I saw five or six Hun trucks going down a road so we began strafing them. Two trucks were left burning. From here we worked inland but ran into a bit of flak near an airdrome, which caused my flight to split up. For some reason they were unable to reform with me, so I continued alone, hoping to pick up the flight on course. At this time I heard on the R/T that Seldom Squadron was in a fight and needed some help, so I dropped my bombs on a small railroad yard, getting direct hits, and then proceeded toward the fight. As I was coming into the area, I saw six Me 109s at 11 o'clock just under the cloud. I edged up in the lower levels of the cloud base and headed toward them. As I came near I saw that two of them were a little behind the four, so I pulled up in the cloud and flew until approximately over the enemy aircraft, then let down. I came out in good position behind the two and managed to grab onto the tail-end Charlie. I made a couple of turns with him and shot a good deflection (something rare in this family). I scored hits and saw the glycol smoke come out. He immediately straightened out of the turn and started down. I was about to follow but the four Me 109s had come in by this time. Then the fun started. Brother, believe me, they can turn when they have a good pilot. I heard the rat-tat-tat of machine guns (and they weren't mine). Through my mirror I did see him squinting down the gun barrel and cursing his poor shooting. This went on for about five years of my future life that I will never live.

Then I started really working. I flipped over at l,000 feet and went down. He must have thought that he had finished me off because he gave me about two seconds to get up into the cloud. Oh, why didn't I get into the cloud to begin with? Well, you try it when the boys are turning deflection on you and let me know how. Back to the 109 that I had shot: I happened to see him auger into a bunch of trees that came conveniently in front of him.

Well, I climbed up to 8,000 feet and headed back toward the area where the previous fight had been reported. By this time I saw a couple of P-47s, so I gathered them in and loved them dearly. Gosh, it was good to see friendly people. Then as we were passing over Evreux airdrome, I saw two Me 109s diving down across the field. We three winged over to the left and tagged onto the two Jerrys. They split as we came in—one going to the low left and the other high right. I took the left one, leaving the right one to the other boys—this Me was a bit easier. He must have seen me shoot the other day when I couldn't hit the top soil of France, because he let me shoot a nice deflection. It worked. He smoked, straightened out, let go the canopy and jumped, but the simple b——'s chute didn't open. The plane burst nicely into small bits.

By this time the other boys were having a big go with the other Me. I saw him coming in time to turn into him. As he went past, I saw the Stripes on the fuselage designating him as a leader or Superman or sumpin'. Well, he figured he had enough so he began climbing. He gained about 4,000 on the initial acceleration, but my ol' 47 with both balls out and water in kept behind him. We went from zero up to 20,000 feet, with the 109 just over and ahead of me all the time. However, at 18,000 feet I began to overtake him as his engine began to boil water. His second mistake was when he thought that he would put the nose down and go home. I ran the indicated air speed up to 500 and caught him at 3,000 feet. I shot a long burst as he went into the cloud (I saw a couple of small strikes on the tail). Well, I figured that having gone this far I wouldn't leave now, so I went into the cloud after him. When I came out he was pulling up. He went into a loop and then changed his mind, probably thinking that I would spin, so he made the loop an Immelmann. He had had it then. Strikes began to appear as I was in good range. He let go the canopy and then bailed out. The ship crashed and blew up. I took a picture with the K-25 camera of the chute and the Jerry. I now wish that I had shot the SOB. I claim three Me 109s destroyed and one pilot destroyed.

–*Col. Glenn E. Duncan*

✪Maj. John B. England
17.5 Victories

Capt. John B. England of the 362nd Fighter Squadron, 357th Fighter Group, had 17.5 victories. He was killed in a postwar accident, and England Air Force Base, Louisiana, was named for him. *Olmsted*

John Brooks England was born in Caruthersville, Missouri, on January 15, 1923.

He entered the U.S. Army Air Force's aviation cadet program and graduated from pilot training at Yuma, Arizona, on March 10, 1943. He was assigned to the 362nd Fighter Squadron of the 357th Fighter Group to fly his combat tour.

Flying P-51s his whole career, he downed 17 enemy fighters and shared in the destruction of another.

England stayed in the Air Force after the war and was promoted to lieutenant colonel. He was commanding the 399th Fighter-Bomber Squadron in France when the engine of his F-86 failed on final approach to land on November 17, 1954. Rather than crash into a barracks, he veered off to the side and crashed to his death. England Air Force Base in Alexandria, Louisiana, was named for Lieutenant Colonel England.

Decorations: Silver Star, Distinguished Flying Cross with 4 Oak Leaf Clusters, and Air Medal with 14 Oak Leaf Clusters.

Assigned aircraft in World War II:

P-51 B 42-106462 G4-H, *U've Had It*

P-51 D 44-13735 G4-H, *U've Had it*

P-51D 44-14709 G4-E, *Missouri Armada*

TYPE OF MISSION: Combat
DATE: 6 October 1944
UNIT: 362nd Fighter Squadron, 357th Fighter Group
TIME: 1200 hours
LOCATION OF ACTION: 23 miles northwest of Berlin
WEATHER: CAVU
TYPE OF ENEMY AIRCRAFT ENCOUNTERED: Me 109
CLAIM: Two unknown; Two Me 109s destroyed, One Me 109 damaged

---

I was leading Dryden Group at 23,000 feet, escorting two combat wings of bombers that had just turned on their initial point. About three minutes later I looked back and saw enemy fighters going through two combat wings several miles behind us. I immediately turned and headed for the enemy planes, taking two squadrons along and leaving one squadron to protect our assigned bombers. Before we could reach the harassed bombers, the enemy fighters had made about six company-front passes from the rear and had shot down six of them. In addition to making this type of attack, the enemy planes made passes singly from three o'clock and eight o'clock high from the bombers. The attacks were both aggressive and effective. I believe that if we had reached them only five minutes later, the whole combat wing would have been wiped out.

I caught about six Me 109s coming out of the front of the bombers and tacked on to what I thought was the last man. I began firing from 600 yards and saw strikes on both his wings. Just then tracers began coming over my wings. I broke sharply to the left in time to see a P-51 shooting down an Me 109 that had been on my tail.

Immediately after this I caught another 109 coming out of the bombers and got on his tail. I began firing from 800 yards, closing to 200 yards, using my K-14 gun sight for 50-degree deflection shots. I observed numerous strikes on his wing roots and cockpit. The pilot jettisoned his canopy, but I did not see him get out. However, my wingman called that the pilot bailed out and that I should break off my attack. I watched the 109 spin downward, crash, and explode.

By this time I had worked down to 12,000 feet. I climbed up to the bombers just in time to catch three Me 109s making an attack from seven o'clock high. I was alone, but decided to break the attack. I turned into the enemy aircraft and began shooting at the second man from very close range at a 40- to 50-degree deflection. The other two planes split-essed to the deck, but this one went into a very tight Lufbery with me. I got strikes on his engine and left wing tip. The pilot bailed out on the second turn of the Lufbery, jumping out toward the inside of the turn. His engine must have quit, or he would have had no reason to bail out that soon. I saw his chute open. I claim two Me 109s destroyed and one Me 109 damaged.

Ammunition: 750 rounds expended

–*Capt. John B. England*

This was Capt. England's final aircraft, *Missouri Armada*. Note very unusual OD finish for this period of the war. *Olmsted*

```
TYPE OF MISSION: Combat
DATE: 14 January 1945
UNIT: 362nd Fighter Squadron, 357th Fighter Group
TIME: 1240 B.S.T.
LOCATION OF ACTION: 20 miles northwest of Berlin
WEATHER: CAVU
TYPE OF ENEMY AIRCRAFT ENCOUNTERED: Me 109
CLAIM: One Me 109 destroyed, one pilot killed
```

I was leading Potent Dollar Squadron, which was top cover for the escort of Vinegrove 1-1, 1-2, 1-3. At 1240 hours a large gaggle of about 100 enemy aircraft approached the bombers from 12 o'clock high. The enemy aircraft seemed to hesitate in making an initial attack. They made several orbits as though they were sizing the situation up. This was to our advantage. While they were "orbiting," I placed my squadron in the proper position and at the same time headed toward the enemy aircraft, hoping to break up the gaggle before they could attack the bombers. They did start an attack before we could get to them, but we interfered slightly and engaged the Krauts in individual dogfights.

I caught one Me 109 that slipped through and started toward the bombers. I got on his tail but was out of firing range. The pilot displayed a little judgment by looking around; then he put his ship in a 90-degree vertical dive from 32,000 feet. I followed him down. At about every 5,000 feet during the descent he would roll and do some violent evasive maneuvers. I just did a tight spiral around him. At 8,000 feet he made a very tight pull-out and leveled off. Evidently the pilot thought he had lost me, for he began flying straight and level. Maybe he didn't realize the speed of the .50 caliber bullet and decided to take time out for a decision. I made a little tighter pull-out and started firing at 200 yards closing to 50 yards. I got strikes all over the left side and the left wing.

Just before I released the trigger, about 4 feet of the left wing ripped off. The pilot did not get out as his ship went into the ground, making a big explosion. The pilot had been fair, but he had made the usual mistake that prevents fair pilots from becoming good pilots.

Our squadron racked up a wonderful score that day and established further proof that good spirit, good formation, discipline, and teamwork pay dividends. The wingmen did fine work, and only one pilot returned home alone. I claim one Me 109 destroyed (Air).

Ammunition: 240 rounds expended

—Maj. John B. England

✪Lt. Col. Robert W. Foy
15 Victories

Capt. Robert W. Foy of the 363rd Fighter Squadron, 357th Fighter Group, and one of his earlier aircraft, *Reluctant Rebel*. Foy would score 15 victories in his two tours with the 357th. *USAAF*

Robert William Foy was born on March 13, 1916, in New York.

Foy entered flight training with the U.S. Army Air Force and graduated as a pilot on May 20, 1943. He joined the 363rd Fighter Squadron of the 357th Fighter Group at the end of January 1944 and flew two combat tours with the group. He scored seven of his victories on his first tour.

Following World War II Foy went to work for North American Aviation and also flew with the California National Guard. He was on an assignment for North American when he was killed in an airplane accident in a B-25 on March 25, 1950.

Decorations: Silver Star, Distinguished Flying Cross with 2 Oak Leaf Clusters, and Air Medal with 18 Oak Leaf Clusters.

Assigned aircraft in World War II:

P-51D 44-13717 B6-V, *Reluctant Rebel*

P-51D 44-6321 B6-V, *Little Shrimp*

```
⚙ TYPE OF MISSION:Combat                                    ⚙
  DATE:29 June 1944
  UNIT:363rd Fighter Squadron, 357th Fighter Group
  TIME:0905 hours
  LOCATION OF ACTION:Southwest Leipzig
  WEATHER:High clear-low haze-5/10 cover
  TYPE OF ENEMY AIRCRAFT ENCOUNTERED:MFW 190,
  Me 109
  CLAIM:Three destroyed: One FW 190, and two Me 109s
⚙                                                            ⚙
```

I was leading Cement Green flight, escorting bombers southwest of Leipzig when four FW 190s attacked my flight from nine o'clock high. They fired and passed over the top of my flight, making a turn left to cut us off. I called for Cement Blue to break right and I put 20-degree flaps down and cut my throttle, maneuvering to the rear of the enemy aircraft, which were at the time in string. I pulled up on the tail of the rear FW 190, which started to turn to the left. I followed him in a Lufbery, firing with about a two-radii lead. I observed strikes all over the fuselage and wings, at which time he straightened out in level flight and bailed out, along with the debris that was flying from his ship. Immediately after breaking off the attack of the FW 190, I saw a P-51 being chased by an Me 109 just off at about three o'clock to me and low. I pulled up and dived onto the tail of the Me 109, pulling up below his tail. I followed him for about 15 seconds in close trail with him and below. I pulled and fired two short bursts, observing strikes on his right wing and beneath the fuselage. The Me 109 immediately broke to the left, did one rather fast roll, and the pilot bailed out. The pilot's chute did not open.

Little Shrimp was Maj. Robert Foy's mount on his second tour with the 357th Group. He scored eight of his victories, including an Me 262, on his second tour. *USAAF*

I called my wingman and received no answer. I then called my second element leader, who replied that he had lost sight of me after I had destroyed the FW 190 and went after the Me 109. I was pulled into a sharp left turn and saw a ship on my tail. I pulled into a tighter turn and started to spin into the overcast, recovering after about two turns. I pulled my flaps down, cut my throttle, and continued turning to the left. I had completed about three-fourths of a 360 turn when the Me 109 cut across in front of me at a fast rate of speed. I pulled up my flaps and gave it full throttle and full rpm, pulsing up on his tail, low and in trail. I fired one burst, observing strikes on the right wing. The enemy aircraft did a split-ess, and I followed in a split-ess. He pulled out of range in a vertical dive. I glanced at my airspeed, which indicated well over 550 miles per hour. The Me 109 was still pulling away from me. I pulled out at 3,000 feet and the Me 109 was still in a vertical. I climbed up to 6,000 feet and circled the immediate area. I did not see the enemy aircraft hit the ground, but there was a spot on the ground in that area which looked as if either a bomb or an airplane had gone in. I claim one FW 190, two Me 109s destroyed.

Ammunition expended: 514 rounds

–Capt. Robert W. Foy

✪Lt. Col. Francis S. Gabreski

28 Victories

Lt. Col. Francis "Gabby" Gabreski, when his score was around 15. This would have been in the spring of 1944. He would go on to score 28 times in the air and become the top ace of the Eighth Air Force. *USAAF*

Francis Stanley Gabreski was born in Oil City, Pennsylvania, on January 28, 1919. He was a premed student at Notre Dame University when he entered the U.S. Army Air Corps as an aviation cadet on July 20, 1940. He graduated from flight training and received his wings at Maxwell Field, Alabama, on March 14, 1941. Gabreski was a pilot assigned to the 45th Pursuit Squadron at Wheeler Field, Hawaii, when the Japanese struck on December 7, 1941.

In October 1942, Gabreski was transferred to England to become liaison officer to a Polish Air Force fighter squadron. When the 56th Fighter Group arrived in England, he was transferred to the 61st Fighter Squadron of that unit. He remained with the 56th Group and became the top Eighth Air Force fighter ace with 28 aerial victories. He struck a knoll while strafing a German airfield on July 20, 1944, and was forced to crash-land. He was taken prisoner shortly thereafter and held in Stalag Luft I at Barth, Germany, until the end of the war in Europe.

Gabreski was released from the Army Air Force in September 1946, but returned to active duty in April 1947. Gabreski served first in the Fourth Fighter Wing during the Korean Conflict and then took over command of the 51st Fighter Wing. During his combat tour from June 1951 to June 1952, he was credited with the destruction of 6.5 MiG 15s. The balance of Gabreski's career was spent largely with tactical fighter wings.

He retired as colonel and commander of the 52nd Fighter Wing in October 1967. Following his retirement, Gabreski joined Grumman Aerospace Corporation, and later served several years as president of the Long Island Railroad. Gabreski now resides in retirement at his long-time home on Long Island, New York.

Decorations: (World War II): Distinguished Service Cross, Silver Star with Oak Leaf Cluster, Distinguished Flying Cross with 9 Oak Leaf Clusters, Air Medal with 4 Oak Leaf Clusters, Bronze Star Medal, British Distinguished Flying Cross, Polish Cross of Valor, French Legion of Honor and Croix de Guerre with Palm, and Belgian Croix de Guerre; (Korea): Distinguished Service Medal, Distinguished Flying Cross with 2 Oak Leaf Clusters, and Air Medal with 2 Oak Leaf Clusters.

Known aircraft flown in World War II:

P-47D 42-7871 HV-A

P-47D 42-8458 HV-F

P-47D 42-25510 HV-A

P-47D 42-25864 HV-A

```
TYPE OF MISSION: Combat
DATE: 22 May 1944
UNIT: 61st Fighter Squadron, 56th Fighter Group
TIME: 1230-1245 hours
LOCATION OF ACTION: Hoperhofen A/D
WEATHER: 7/10
TYPE OF ENEMY AIRCRAFT ENCOUNTERED: FW 190
CLAIM: Three FW 190s destroyed, one FW 190 probably
destroyed
```

Leading Whippet Squadron and flying Whippet White One, the group made rendezvous over Dummer Lake at 1215. The squadrons fanned out with the Whippet Squadron, proceeding on a vector 30 degrees, which took us about 20 miles east of Bremen. From an altitude of 20,000 feet, obscured by 8/10 cloud coverage, two locomotives were seen steaming from Bremen. Yellow flight was ordered to take the bounce while the remaining three flights let down to 15,000 feet and remained circling over the target. While in this circle a very well camouflaged airdrome appeared beneath us. Upon closer observation there seemed to be quite a bit of activity below. At this moment, Yellow flight called in aircraft taking off from this particular airdrome. Sure enough, about 16 FW 190s were seen taking off line abreast. Immediately the three flights let down and took the bounce. By the time White flight got into position for a dead-astern attack, the enemy planes picked up enough speed and altitude to give us a damn good fight. The battle started at about 3,000 feet. I took my flight ahead to attack a section of eight FW 190s flying pretty good formation, while about 10 to 12 FW 190s were left to the second and third flights directly behind us. I closed in on the first FW 190, opened fire at range, and saw hits all over the fuselage and wings. The plane fell off to the side and burst into flames while I pulled up for the second kill. I opened up within range, saw hits over the fuselage, and the plane broke off to the side,

Lt. Col. Francis Gabreski and his crew chief near the end of his combat career in the ETO. While strafing, he struck a knoll with his propeller and was forced to crash-land. He would spend the rest of the war as a POW. *USAAF*

burning badly. The canopy flew open and the Hun bailed out.

While still following this ship down, I looked behind and saw myself wedged between two Huns coming in for the kill. I broke right for all that I was worth and made about two orbits with the Hun before I was able to outclimb the 190. It was at this moment that I saw a P-47 going down in flames and another smoking very badly. This short of shook me, so I regained about 12,000 feet of altitude and asked the squadron to rendezvous above the airfield. After circling for about five minutes I managed to get six planes together. No sooner had the planes reformed when 20-plus FW 190s were sighted headed across the airdrome in very good formation.

The boys on the airfield threw up everything but the kitchen sink. The Huns' formation blew up, one flight going right and the other ships breaking formation and climbing for all they were worth. A green flare was fired from one of the ships and the ground guns ceased firing. This was our cue. The six of us dove from 12,000 feet and picked individual targets. I picked a flight of six to my right, flying a pretty string formation. I closed to within range of the last man and opened fire, seeing hits around the fuselage and wings. The plane lost speed rapidly, trailing volumes of black smoke, then rolled over and hit the ground. Closing to about 500 yards of the second man from the end and still holding fire, since ammunition was precious at a moment like this, I glanced to my left and saw an FW 190 just beneath my left wing rapidly falling behind and trying to get into position for an astern shot. I cut my throttle, drew back on the stick and practically stalled the plane. The Hun overran me and I fell behind him but in no position to fire. The FW 190 went into a very tight right-hand turn with about five FW 190s the same out in front. After about three turns with six Huns in a Lufbery, I broke up in a very steep climbing turn. At this moment another FW 190 came down on me from above and got a 60-degree deflection shot at me. I kept climbing and turning till I got to 10,000 feet. Looking about, I saw a few friendly fighters about the sky, so I joined up and headed for home with four ships.

On vector for five minutes, Blue 3 called in about 20-plus a short distance northeast of Bremen. The five of us made a 180 and headed in the direction of Hamburg. As I arrived over the area of our last battle I spotted a lone FW 190 flying down on the deck. I lost him under the overcast, so I flew over the cloud and waited at the other end, circling. I picked up my target again and made the bounce, full dead astern of the Hun at 3,000 feet. Just below the overcast I closed to range and opened fire. My first burst was a little high, but the second connected, with hits near the wing roots and fuselage. The plane appeared to snap down and when last seen was rolling off to the left, pouring out what appeared to be oil and black smoke. I pulled up above the overcast and headed home. I claim three FW 190s destroyed and one FW 190 probably destroyed.

Ammunition: 1,419 rounds expended (.50-caliber API)

−Lt. Col. Francis S. Gabreski

```
TYPE OF MISSION: Combat
DATE: 7 June 1944
UNIT: 61st Fighter Squadron, 56th Fighter Group
TIME: 1240 hours
LOCATION OF ACTION: East of Dreux
WEATHER: 9/10 clouds
TYPE OF ENEMY AIRCRAFT ENCOUNTERED: Me 109
and FW 190
CLAIM: One Me 109 destroyed and one FW 190 destroyed
```

Leading Whippet Squadron and flying Whippet White One, the squadron proceeded to Chartres and dive-bombed a railroad line. Returning by the way of Dreux airdrome, the squadron circled the drome at 10,000 feet. Upon completing the orbit, two planes were picked up flying on the deck. Two flights let down through the hole in the clouds, and White flight headed in pursuit of two FW 190s. Just as we reached about 2,000 feet I looked up to nine o'clock and saw 20-plus aircraft flying in beautiful formation. Upon first glance I assumed that they were Spitfires, but upon closer investigation I learned that they were Me 109s and FW 190s. I broke off my first attack, called the gaggle in, and attacked the first two Me 109s. One saw me closing in dead astern and he broke; the second kept on a vector until I started firing and then went into a left-hand turn. I kept firing within range and saw just a few hits around the tail section. At that moment the Me 109 seemed to have lost power as I overran him. I cut my throttle, pulled up, and just as I was about to go down on the same Me 109 and finish him off, I saw the pilot bail out. His chute opened at about 2,000 feet.

I began regaining my altitude, when I saw about four FW 190s a little to the right and about 1,000 feet below. I shoved everything forward and it was some time before I was able close within range. Just before the 190 dove into the haze at 2,000 to 3,000 feet, I corrected my deflection just as I closed within range and saw hits all over the fuselage and a slight explosion with fire emerging from the fuselage. The plane fell off to the left and went into the ground. Lieutenant Gladlych saw the plane hit the ground. I claim one Me 109 and one FW 190 destroyed.

—Lt. Col. Francis S. Gabreski

```
TYPE OF MISSION:Combat
DATE:12 June 1944
UNIT:61st Fighter Squadron, 56th Fighter Group
TIME:1525 hours
LOCATION OF ACTION:Vicinity of Evreux
WEATHER:1/10 cumulus clouds
TYPE OF ENEMY AIRCRAFT ENCOUNTERED:Me 109
CLAIM:Two Me 109s destroyed
```

Leading the group and flying Whippet One, the group penetrated to the vicinity of Paris. After patrolling for about half an hour, the group received word from Colgate that the 353rd Group was engaged west of Paris. At the moment we were headed north about 10 miles east of Paris. The group immediately changed vector and headed west until we reached the point of combat. No enemy aircraft were seen in the vicinity, so we proceeded on our uneventful tour between Chartres and Beauvis. Just as we were about to head out in the vicinity of Evreux,

Whippet Red 3 called in a few planes flying north along the deck. I couldn't pick them up, so I was advised to make a 180 left, and they would be directly below me. Sure enough, a 180 was executed, and 12 Me 109s appeared ahead of me flying a beautiful abreast formation at 9,000 feet. I immediately dove from 14,000 feet and closed on one Me 109 flying a wing position at 3,000 feet. My closing speed was terrific. Just about range I opened fire and held it until I closed to nought feet. There were strikes all over the ventral side of the fuselage and tail section. Pieces flew off the aircraft and flames billowed from the midventral section of the fuselage. I barely avoided colliding with the Me 109. As I pulled underneath this plane I was forced to shove the stick forward for all that I was worth as the 109 fell, nose-heavy.

I regained my altitude to the left and lost practically all my speed when I reversed the turn and spotted four more 109s still flying in pretty good formation quite a distance ahead and beneath me. Applying full throttle, I dove from about 6,000 feet and intercepted an Me 109 just as the flight of four was breaking up. My target went into a steep right-hand turn and I followed and opened fire in range. Hits were seen over the fuselage and cockpit. I closed to nought feet and fell to the outside of the Me 109 when the plane fell off to the left and I barely avoided ramming it. The plane fell off burning, while I made a left-hand circuit and started climbing.

Just at this moment, I looked back to clear my tail and I saw an Me 109 closing in on me from below. I kept climbing and orbiting left while the Hun, just a little out of range, kept firing at me. This lasted for about a half minute before another Thunderbolt came to my rescue. As the Thunderbolt headed down on the Me 109, the Hun rolled over and dove away, thanks to my good comrade, Lieutenant Heaton.

A note of interest: It is my opinion that some 109s have only one gun firing through the hub of the prop as their only armament. At least the 109 firing at me had but one gun. Perhaps the Hun believes in maneuverability and climb, and as a result may sacrifice armament. I claim two Me 109s destroyed.

Ammunition: 564 rounds expended (.50-caliber API)

—Lt. Col. Francis S. Gabreski

```
TYPE OF MISSION: Combat
DATE: 5 July 1944
UNIT: 61st Fighter Squadron, 56th Fighter Group
TIME: 1600 hours
LOCATION OF ACTION: Evreux
WEATHER: 8/10 low cumulus
TYPE OF ENEMY AIRCRAFT ENCOUNTERED: Me 109
CLAIM: One Me 109 destroyed
```

I was flying Whippet White One and leading the group. We made rendezvous with the bombers and escorted uneventfully to the Evreux area. Just as the group was about to break off escort, a lone Me 109 was seen on the deck flying east. I made my bounce but lost him as I went through the broken cloud layer at 5,000 feet. I made one orbit beneath the clouds and regained my altitude. In the meantime, my Red flight leader saw many enemy aircraft near an airdrome and he engaged a few Me 109s. Circling above the layer of clouds, I saw an Me 109 being pursued by a P-47. Since I had altitude I decided to take the bounce, but just as I was closing in I saw the P-47 fire, getting hits all over the Me 109. The Hun evaded into the clouds while the P-47 broke off. I in turn went through the cloud to get in on the kill as the Hun broke out of the layer of cumulus. Still out of range, I saw the Hun bail out and the plane hit the ground. Returning to base I learned that Lieutenant Lanowski was responsible for the de-

This is Lt. Col. Francis Gabreski's last Thunderbolt, taken shortly after D-Day. Note the invasion stripes and center line drop tank. *USAAF*

struction of this particular aircraft. Once again I regained my altitude and circled. On the deck once more, I saw three Me 109s. I made a bounce, overran them, and from there combat ensued. As I was closing in on about two Me 109s diving away, I saw a lone Hun climbing to the left, so I broke off my initial attack and wound it up with the one Hun. After about three turns at about 3,000 feet I got in a few bursts, but without results. My firing must have shook the Hun, as he dove to the deck in a straight line. I closed in very rapidly. Still a bit out of range, the Hun made a left-hand turn. I gave him about two rings of deflection, which put him out of my sight. I pressed the trigger and let the Hun fly into sight. The Me 109 was smoking very badly. The Hun leveled off and I closed in for the kill, getting hits all over the fuselage. I broke off my attack after overrunning. Before completing a 180 turn, I saw the pilot's chute open at about 200 feet off the ground, while the plane crashed into an open field. I claim one Me 109 destroyed.

Ammunition: 750 rounds expended (.50-caliber API)

—Lt. Col. Francis S. Gabreski

```
TYPE OF MISSION: Combat
DATE: 29 November 1943
UNIT: 61st Fighter Squadron, 56th Fighter Group
TIME: 1425-1440
LOCATION OF ACTION: Northeast of Bremen
WEATHER: 7/10 cirrus below 24,000 feet
TYPE OF ENEMY AIRCRAFT ENCOUNTERED: Me 109
CLAIM: Two Me 109s destroyed
```

I was flying Keyworth White One. We made landfall at approximately 1345 hours (solid overcast) and rendezvoused with big friends at 1411 hours (solid overcast). Keyworth positioned itself on the left side of the Forts at 30,000 feet. The Forts were 1,500 feet below us. At 1425 hours the Forts made a 60-degree, left-hand turn and proceeded to the target. Being on the left and well out to the side, I spotted about 10 FW 190s coming head-on to the bombers. Before I could actually get into position to fire, the enemy planes went down and below the Forts, possibly hitting the lower section of the bombers. All this took place after reaching the API. Just as the bombers approached their target, my Blue section and Red flights were split up as a result of a bounce upon enemy aircraft approaching the bombers from 10 o'clock. I proceeded to investigate vapor trails well out to the side and ahead of the bombers. Much to my surprise, these trails represented 40-plus Me 109s. My wingman, Lieutenant Powers, and I happened to be the only two left of the White flight. I immediately decided to bounce the first eight, who were at 28,000 feet, headed for the bombers. Closing in on the last man, I was suddenly warned by Lieutenant Powers that we were being attacked from astern. I broke off my attack and pointed my nose up in a 45-degree climb. Outclimbing the pursuers two or three times, Lieutenant Powers and I made a determined effort to close in on eight Me 109s just below us at 28,000 feet. Having the advantage in altitude and with full throttle I pointed my nose toward the formation, picked on a straggler, closed in to 600 yards, and fired. I observed hits on the fuselage and belly tank. The belly tank broke up into pieces. I pressed my attack and closed to 200 yards when I observed gray smoke pouring from the engine along with a very little flame. The plane fell off to the left, went into a spin, and was seen going into the clouds. A few seconds elapsed and I swung over to the right, picked out another 109 out of four, opened fire at 700 yards, and closed to about 200 (dead astern). The belly tank blew up and strikes were centered on the fuselage and wings. Smoke and glycol poured out of the engine, while the plane went into a slight dive and flew straight for about 10 seconds. At 24,000 feet the 109 fell off slowly to the left, rolled over, and went straight down into the overcast. Lieutenant Powers and I recovered and headed for home as our petrol was running low. There is nothing like an old reliable wingman, a man that you can depend on. Lieutenant Powers certainly has what it takes. I claim two Me 109s destroyed.

–Maj. Francis S. Gabreski

✪Maj. Don S. Gentile
21.83 Victories

A fine study of two of the top guns of the Fourth Fighter Group. Maj. Don Gentile, on the left, scored 21.83 victories, primarily in Mustangs, while Capt. Duane Beeson scored most of his 17.3 kills flying Thunderbolts. *USAAF*

Dominic Salvatore Gentile was born on December 6, 1920, in Piqua, Ohio.

Gentile was another who could not wait to fly and fight, and so joined the Royal Canadian Air Force in September 1940. Following graduation from pilot training he was sent to England, where he became an instructor. Gentile finally got out of the assignment and joined No. 133 American Eagle Squadron. With No. 133 Squadron he was credited with his first two aerial victories. When the Eagle Squadrons transferred to the U.S. Army Air Force, Gentile went to the 336th Fighter Squadron of the Fourth Fighter Group.

He scored four victories flying the P-47, but when the group got P-51s he began his string of victories. When he was withdrawn from combat, he was a captain, had scored 21.83 aerial victories, and had destroyed another six enemy aircraft on the ground. Gentile returned to the United States in April 1944. His next assignment was as a test pilot at Wright–Patterson Field in Ohio. Gentile left the Air Force in April 1946.

He returned to active duty in 1947 and was assigned to the Pentagon in Washington, D.C. He was killed in an accident on January 28, 1951, while flying a T-33 over Maryland.

Decorations: Distinguished Service Cross with Oak Leaf Cluster, Distinguished Flying Cross with 7 Oak Leaf Clusters, and Air Medal with 3 Oak Leaf Clusters.

Assigned aircraft in World War II:

Spitfire Vb B1255 MD-T, *Buckeye Don*

P-47D 42-8659 VF-T, *Donnie Boy*

P-51D 43-6913 VF-T, *Shangri–La*

```
TYPE OF MISSION: Engagement
DATE: 14 January 1944
UNIT: 336th Fighter Squadron
TIME: 1500-1520 hours
LOCATION OF ACTION: Compiegne Woods. 12,000
(First), Zero feet second
WEATHER: Clear; hazy on deck
TYPE OF ENEMY AIRCRAFT ENCOUNTERED: FW 190
CLAIM: Two FW 190s destroyed
```

I was flying Blue One in Shirtblue Squadron. I saw and reported a gaggle of 15 190s flying east, 3,000 feet below. We were flying south. I took my section down, which included F/O Richards (2), Lieutenant Norley (3), and Lieutenant Garrison (4).

As soon as we went down the 190s split, fan shaped, into two groups. I picked two stragglers flying north and attacked at eight o'clock to the enemy aircraft, which were in a 50-degree dive. I closed in to about 300 yards and fired a long burst at the number-two 190 and observed strikes around the left side of the cockpit, after which I saw smoke coming out. He rolled over (at 8,000 feet) very slowly and went into a spiral dive vertically. He crashed in open country, near woods. Lieutenant Carlson Red (l) and F/O Richards confirm this.

I slid over immediately back of the number-one 190, closed to about 250 yards and started firing, closing to about 150 yards. We were in a very shallow dive from 4,000 feet. I observed strikes around the cockpit and engine. As I was trying to follow him down in his slipstream to get another shot, he hit the woods and I pulled out, just missing the woods myself.

Maj. Don Gentile's *Donnie Boy*, the P-47 that he flew in the early days of the Fourth Fighter Group. Gentile had 4.5 victories in P-47s. *USAAF*

Just as I pulled up, I was jumped by two 190s and the fun really started. The number-one 190 was so close to me that I heard his guns and he hit me. I broke and the first 190 went over me. I stayed in a port turn because the number two was still coming in, but he was not firing. In the meantime the number one had pulled up sharply to position himself for another attack. I quickly swung starboard and fired a short burst at the number two, whom I never saw again. All this action took place at tree-top height. I swung port to get away from the number one man who was firing but giving too much deflection, as his tracer was going in front of me. I used the last of my ammo (except some that had jammed) on the last burst at the number-two FW 190. I was trying to outturn him, but he stayed inside me. I suddenly flicked and just about wiped myself out in the trees. After recovering, I reversed my turn to starboard and there he was, still inside me and still shooting like hell. I kept on turning and skidding—all I could do. He slid under and overshot and I reversed again port. We met head-on and he was still firing. For the next 10 minutes we kept reversing turns from head-on attacks, trying to get on each other's tails. The last time he came in he didn't shoot, so he must have been out of ammunition. He then left, and I felt like getting out and doing the rumba. All my temperatures were in the red, so I climbed up slowly and came home. I claim two FW 190s destroyed. I do not know what happened to the third one I fired at, so I make no claim on him.

—Capt. Don S. Gentile

```
TYPE OF MISSION:Combat
DATE:3 March 1944
UNIT:336th Fighter Squadron
TIME:1130-1150 hours
LOCATION OF ACTION:Witenburg-24,000 to 15,000
feet
WEATHER:5-8/10 medium and low
TYPE OF ENEMY AIRCRAFT ENCOUNTERED:FW 190
Do 217
CLAIM:Two FW 190s destroyed and one Do 217 damaged
```

I was flying Red One in Shirtblue Squadron. Lieutenant Millikan was the only other member of the section. I saw many smoke trails coming up from the south at about 28,000 feet and reported them. The eight of us, at 23,000 feet, turned into them. A group of 110s, Do 217s, and Ju 88s passed underneath us coming head-on. I rolled starboard and started down but was bounced by 10 FW 190s that Lieutenant Millikan, doing an outstanding job, engaged and drove away from me. I dove on down and got on the tail of a twin-engined plane, but my canopy was so badly frosted that I couldn't see anything. I was scared of hitting him, so pulled up and turned on my defroster. When the canopy started to clear, I saw it was an Me 110—right beside me and firing at me. I broke away and was bounced again by 3 FW 190s. I turned into them, met them head-on, and they just kept on going. I then bounced the Do 217 in a port turn, fired a short burst above and astern, and my gunsight went out. I pulled up, gave another short burst, and saw strikes. Just then two FW 190s flashed past me on each side, so I pulled away.

I asked Lieutenant Millikan if he was with me, and he said, "Hell, I'm fighting 10 FWs," so I figured he needed help. I tried to gather the odd Mustang I saw floating around, telling them to join up. Then I saw a gaggle beneath me going around in a pretty good formation. I half-rolled and went down, but suddenly found myself in the midst of 12 to 14 FW 190s, with no Mustangs around. I did a port, steep climb turn, full out. On the way up an FW 190 was in front of me. I pulled around and put him under my nose and fired a burst. I then repeated the process, and saw some pieces come off and the pilot bail out.

Then I was bounced again by four FW 190s, which I met head-on. They fired at me but I didn't return the fire because one of my guns had jammed, and I wanted to save ammo. I kept reversing my turn, trying to tell other Mustangs when to break, when two more 190s came head-on. I broke and tried to get on their tails. I observed eight more coming down on me, so I broke up into them, reversing my turn. They fired, but again I did not. There were two, one of each side of me starting in. I let them get within range, pulled up in a port turn, trying to get them to think I was going to turn into the port 190s, but completed my corkscrew roll, reversing it underneath toward the two on the starboard, just passing at 90 degrees to him and very close. I did not fire. They kept on going. I went down and tried to bounce

Ready to taxi out for another combat mission is Capt. Don Gentile, in his last Mustang, *Shangri-La.* USAAF

another twin, but overshot and pulled up sharply. This maneuver put me right through a formation of three twins, but they were firing at me so I broke away. I continued upward full bore when I saw another 190 in front of me. I pulled my nose through until I thought it was the right deflection and fired a short burst. I repeated firing short bursts the same way until I saw smoke coming from the engine, which was on fire. I pulled up starboard and then back to port and observed the FW 190 going down in a slow spiral, apparently out of control. I last saw him at cloud level (about 4,000 feet) but didn't feel it was healthy to watch any longer or to follow him down, since there were too many Jerrys around.

I then saw three FW 190s off the tail of a Mustang that was pouring smoke. I told him to break, and he did a quick snap and went straight down. I dove down to try and get them off his tail, but couldn't catch them, so I pulled up again. I saw two Mustangs below and discovered they were Major Halsey and Lieutenant Dunn. I called and told them to join up with me when two FWs bounced Major Halsey, closing very fast. I looked up and saw eight more getting positioned to come down on me. I let them bounce me, because I figured I could get the two bouncing Major Halsey before the eight could get me. In the meantime, I kept yelling to Major Halsey to break. Both 190s were firing at me. The major did three snap rolls and I met those four 190s in a frontal quarter attack. Neither of us fired. The 190s flicked at this time and went down. I saw that Major Halsey was OK, but the eight 190s were getting within firing range. I pulled up sharply to meet them and they passed me as I was on my back. They kept going.

I then told Lieutenant Dunn and Major Halsey to join up and they did. We steered 280 degrees, Major Halsey and I ending up at Guernsey. Lieutenant Dunn was having trouble, so I told him I would do a port turn so that he could catch up. In the turn I fell behind him and that's the last I saw of him. We were then at 10,000 feet. I heard Lieutenant Dunn calling for a heading two hours later. I landed on the south coast out of gas. I claim two FW 190s destroyed and one Do 217 damaged.

—Capt. Don S. Gentile

```
TYPE OF MISSION:Combat
DATE:29 March 1944
UNIT:336th Fighter Squadron
TIME:1330 hours
LOCATION OF ACTION:Target Area-Brunswick
WEATHER:7-8/10 low clouds
TYPE OF ENEMY AIRCRAFT ENCOUNTERED:FW 190,
Me 109
CLAIM:Two FW 190s destroyed and one Me 109 destroyed
```

I was flying Blue One in Shirtblue Squadron at 27,000 feet. I bounced a gaggle of seven or eight FW 190s underneath the bombers, at 17,000 to 18,000 feet. When they saw us, they went down in a spiral dive. I bounced the nearest FW 190 (they were flying line astern), closed to 300 yards, fired, and saw strikes around the cockpit. He rolled over in a port turn slowly and went vertically down. By this time I was at 5,000 to 6,000 feet, indicating close to 500 moving over 400 miles per hour.

I started to level out below the clouds, and Lieutenant Godfrey told me to break because there were two behind me. One of them was firing. I broke and evaded them. I made a tight port orbit, blacking out. When I recovered, there was an FW 190 in front of me, so I closed to about 300 yards and fired. I saw smoke come out and a few pieces flew off. Then the pilot bailed out at l,000–2,000 feet.

I made a tight, climbing spiral to port and climbed to 10,000 feet through a hole in the cloud. I told another Mustang to join up, and we started toward the bombers again. The Mustang with me was attacked by two Me 109s. I told him to break, but apparently he did not hear me, for he continued to fly straight and level. I broke into the 109s, which half-rolled and went into cloud. The Mustang was no longer in sight, but he hadn't been hit and I found out later that he got home OK. I was bounced by another 109 and broke port into him. Just as he started to disappear behind me, I reversed my turn to the starboard and fell astern of him. When I fired, glycol started streaming out and the pilot bailed out. Altitude was 7,000–8,000 feet and range was about 300 yards. I joined the bombers along, later finding some Mustangs, and came home. I claim two FW 190s and one Me 109 destroyed.

–*Capt. Don S. Gentile*

✪Maj. James A. Goodson
14 Victories

Maj. James A. Goodson of the Fourth Fighter Group, a 14-victory ace, was apparently camera shy. You don't find a lot of photos of him. Perhaps he was one of the superstitious ones. *USAAF*

James Alexander Goodson was born on March 21, 1921, in New York City.

When World War II broke out, Goodson went to England and trained as a pilot in the Royal Air Force. He became a member of No. 133 Squadron, one of the American Eagle Squadrons. When the Eagle Squadrons transferred to the U.S. Army Air Corps in September 1942, Goodson became a member of the 336th Fighter Squadron, Fourth Fighter Group. When the unit converted from Spitfires to P-47 Thunderbolts, there was much regret with the pilots. Goodson was one of the pilots who became an ace in the P-47, scoring his first five victories in the aircraft. He was serving as commander of the 336th Fighter Squadron when he was downed by flak on a strafing mission on June 20, 1944. He would spend the rest of World War II in a German prison camp.

Goodson was promoted to lieutenant colonel before he left the U.S. Army Air Corps after the war. As an executive, Goodson was American representative for several companies before he became a vice president for IT&T, based in Belgium.

Goodson now resides in England in retirement.

Decorations: Distinguished Service Cross, Silver Star, Distinguished Flying Cross with 8 Oak Leaf Clusters, and Air Medal with 3 Oak Leaf Clusters.

Assigned aircraft in World War II:
P-47D 42-7959 VF-W
P-51B 43-24848 VF-B
P-51B 43-6895 VF-B
P-51D 44-13303 VF-B

```
TYPE OF MISSION: Combat
DATE: 16 August 1943
UNIT: 336th Fighter Squadron
TIME: 1000 hours
LOCATION OF ACTION: Paris area
WEATHER: Good
TYPE OF ENEMY AIRCRAFT ENCOUNTERED: FW 190
CLAIM: Two FW 190s destroyed
```

While leading Red Section above and on the port of two B-17s, I observed several enemy aircraft about to make a head-on attack on the bombers and led Red Section down. Due to the steep attack, we overshot the first FW 190 but both Red Two (Lieutenant Carlson) and myself fired and we observed hits. This 190 had a yellow nose and yellow tail plane and had bulges under the wings—presumably underslung cannon. This enemy aircraft dove away. I confirm Lieutenant Carlson's claim of one FW 190 damaged.

At this time another FW 190 crossed below and in front of us, turning to make an astern attack on the bombers. I closed to dead line astern and about 75 yards or less. I observed many strikes, saw the enemy aircraft roll on its back, and I followed until I saw him crash straight in a woods north of Paris. I claim this FW 190 destroyed.

While climbing up again with Red Two, another FW 190 crossed in front of us, making an astern attack on the bombers. I fired dead line astern from 250 yards and closed, making many strikes, including a violent flash in the cockpit. The enemy aircraft rolled over and went down in a spin, trailing smoke. I followed him down, squirting when my sights were on, until I had to pull up, at 10,000 feet. I claim this FW 190 destroyed.

—1st Lt. James A. Goodson

```
TYPE OF MISSION:Combat
DATE:29 March 1944
UNIT:336th Fighter Squadron
TIME:1400 hours
LOCATION OF ACTION:Northeast of Brunswick
WEATHER:6/10 at 5,000 feet
TYPE OF ENEMY AIRCRAFT ENCOUNTERED:Ju 88
CLAIM:Two Ju 88s destroyed
```

I led Shirtblue Squadron down on 20-plus enemy aircraft that were approaching the lead box of bombers from two o'clock. As soon as we attacked, the enemy aircraft went into a steep spiral dive, dodging in and out of a cloud. During this chase, my windscreen and, finally, my whole cockpit frosted up, leaving me on instruments at 1,000 feet. When I was able to scratch some of the ice off, I found myself near an airdrome of Ju 88s, with some in the circuit. I attacked one going in for a landing with considerable deflection. I got strikes, but he continued to land. I came back and hit him again as he was taxiing and started him smoking, but due to the frosted condition of my windscreen it was not until after the fourth pass that I considered him blazing sufficiently to call him destroyed. I then observed another 88 flying around. I had trouble getting behind him but finally got a few strikes on him from 90 degrees. He was very close to the deck, and promptly crashed in a field. Although it was a good prang, I returned and got many strikes on it, leaving the crash burning. I claim these two Ju 88s destroyed.

–Maj. James A. Goodson

```
TYPE OF MISSION:Combat
DATE:25 May 1944
UNIT:336th Fighter Squadron
TIME:1000 hours
LOCATION OF ACTION:Strasbourg
WEATHER:Slight haze to 3,000 feet
TYPE OF ENEMY AIRCRAFT ENCOUNTERED:FW 190
CLAIM:One FW 190 destroyed
```

While leading the group on bomber escort to Saaruemines, I took two actions to skirt the bombers in order to intercept any fighters that might come in from the east. We saw a few fighters to the east and immediately went to investigate. These fighters turned out to be 20-plus FW 190s with some 30-plus Me 109s above as top cover. We split them up, but due to the fact that we were outnumbered (50 to 8) we were not able to destroy any. In the ensuing dogfight, my wingman and myself ended up alone on the deck. As I started to climb up, I observed 24 Me 109s and FW 190s (190s predominating) in close formation in six stacks

Maj. James Goodson's aircraft. Goodson had a nice scoreboard, but no personal emblems adorned his plane. *USAAF*

of four line astern (P-51 formation). I told my wingman we would try to sneak up behind and knock off the last section, and try to run away in the haze. As we were closing on the last section, all the Huns broke and a lengthy dogfight ensued with the FW 190s, who showed amazing fighting ability and aggressiveness. It was only after most violent maneuvering and excessive use of throttle and flaps that I was able to get good strikes on the most persistent 190. He pulled up and bailed out, and I took a picture of him bailing. I claim this FW 190 destroyed, confirmed by Lieutenant Grounds (my wingman).

Since the fight had lasted some time and gas was getting low, I collected my wingman and we got away, using full bore and taking advantage of the slight haze.

–Maj. James A. Goodson

✪Lt. Ralph K. Hofer
15 Victories

When he came to the Fourth Fighter Group after training with the RCAF and RAF, Flight Officer Ralph "Kid" Hofer flew a P-47 named for his home state. *USAAF*

Ralph K. Hofer was born in Salem, Missouri, on June 22 , 1921.

Hofer ventured into Canada and joined the Royal Canadian Air Force in July 1941. He graduated from flight training and was sent to England in October 1942.

In June 1943 Hofer transferred to the U.S. Army Air Force as a flight officer and reported to the Fourth Fighter Group. While with the 334th Fighter Squadron he amassed quite a combat record, but he presented his leaders with numerous problems due to his tendency to wander off alone. His promotions came slowly due to his behavior, but he was finally commissioned a second lieutenant in April 1944. While participating in the first shuttle mission to Russia, Hofer was lost while strafing an airfield in Yugoslavia on July 2, 1944.

Decorations: Distinguished Flying Cross with 6 Oak Leaf Clusters, and Air Medal with 3 Oak Leaf Clusters.

Assigned aircraft in World War II:

P-47C 41-5484 QP-L, *The Missouri Kid-Sho Me*

P-51B 42-106924 QP-L, *Salem Representative*

```
TYPE OF MISSION:Combat
DATE:18 March 1944
UNIT:334th Fighter Squadron
TIME:1335 hours
LOCATION OF ACTION:Southeast Mannheim area
WEATHER:Poor visibility
TYPE OF ENEMY AIRCRAFT ENCOUNTERED:Me 109
CLAIM:Two Me 109s destroyed
```

I was flying Pectin White Four to Lieutenant Montgomery. Because my radio was out of service, I did not hear the bounce on 10 enemy aircraft. Following Lieutenant Montgomery down and seeing a good bounce on an Me 109, I turned right, dropped my wing tanks, and dived after him. I saw strikes and an explosion, with pieces flying off. This aircraft started falling with black smoke pouring out. I followed him down through the clouds but lost sight of him. An explosion and a fire were seen near the airdrome, presumably from this enemy aircraft.

On this airdrome, I saw a four-engine aircraft I thought looked like a Liberator. Climbing back up I attempted a bounce on a Me 109 but stall-turned and dived in getting in position. This enemy aircraft went into the clouds but popped up through again. The canopy of this enemy aircraft was jettisoned and the pilot bailed out. Major Goodson confirmed this aircraft.

I then bounced another 109 with belly tank and followed him through the clouds but lost him. I orbited an airdrome but saw nothing. I climbed back up and everybody had left. I then set course for target. Just before arriving, two 109s passed in front of and above me. I climbed up, full throttle, into their smoke trails and got within 600 yards. My prop ran away, and I lost flying speed. A terrific amount of boost and rpm was recorded. I set course for Switzerland at 6,000 feet and in passing Lake Constance, I watched our big friends clobber what looked to be an assembly plant with over 100 enemy aircraft parked in deep snow. I observed many bursts on buildings but not many among aircraft.

I passed into Switzerland and started to climb up to bail out. With a roar, my prop came back to normal, probably due to change of angle. I then averaged up my gas and decided that I could possibly make it back with a little luck. I then watched three 109s shoot a Mustang down before I could help. I then came home, landing at Manston with six gallons of gas.

—Flight Officer Ralph K. Hofer

```
TYPE OF MISSION: Combat
DATE: 1 April 1944
UNIT: 335th Fighter Squadron
TIME: 1040 hours
LOCATION OF ACTION: Northwest of Lake Constance
WEATHER: 6/10 cumulus
TYPE OF ENEMY AIRCRAFT ENCOUNTERED: Me 109
CLAIM: One Me 109 destroyed
```

I was flying Greenbelt Blue Four. We rendezvoused with the bombers at approximately 1030 hours (bombers at 20,000 feet and fighters at 24,000) and started home. Four Huns were reported shooting at a Lib. I saw the Lib going down smoking to my port. Four 109s came in below me after the Lib. I jammed things forward and dived to attack, telling the men with me to get the straggling Hun. I closed in on the other three at about 16,000 feet. I fired a 20-degree deflection shot at 250-yard range, hitting the Hun in the engine and cockpit. Pieces flew off, and glycol started streaming from its radiators. The aircraft then quit flying forward and began to fill with smoke, flames and glycol streaming back. I pulled up behind the number-two man and started firing at 150-yard range but saw no strikes on the enemy aircraft. He saw me and rolled over on his back and dived away.

I followed, closing fast but my aircraft flicked and stalled, and I lost control due to having too much gas in the back tank. When I recovered, the Hun had gone. I joined up with Lieutenant Tussey and came home.

—Flight Officer Ralph K. Hofer

When Flight Officer Hofer got going in the Fourth Fighter Group, he ran up a score quickly. However, his leader had trouble keeping him in formation. Yet he went on to score 15 victories. Here he is with his dog on his personal aircraft, *Salem Representative,* named for his hometown.

```
TYPE OF MISSION: Combat
DATE: 24 May 1944
UNIT: 334th Fighter Squadron
TIME: 1125 hours
LOCATION OF ACTION: East Hamburg district
WEATHER: Hazy
TYPE OF ENEMY AIRCRAFT ENCOUNTERED: FW 190
CLAIM: Two FW 190s destroyed
```

I was flying Cobweb White Three and had rendezvoused with the bombers when 30-plus bandits at 35,000 feet were sighted, coming in at 12 o'clock to us. We had climbed up to 30,000 feet when I sighted four Me 109s come in below us. I attacked but lost sight of them in the haze. I pulled up and sighted three FW 109s attacking a B-17 that was returning. We bounced, and I started shooting, trying to scare them off but they didn't seem to see me; finally I closed on one, getting strikes. The aircraft started smoking, the hood was jettisoned, and the pilot bailed. The other two broke up to the left.

I pulled up to see Lieutenant Fraser, my wingman, behind the other two FW 190s; one made a split-ess with Lieutenant Fraser following. I then broke into the leader, preventing him from firing at Lieutenant Fraser. He did a split-ess, and I followed at 14,000 feet. I got a few scattered hits, and at 10,000 feet, below the clouds, I got more strikes in a tight turn. He pulled sharply up into a cloud and jettisoned his hood. I did not see the pilot bail out, but the aircraft crashed in a field, burning, and its ammo exploding at intervals. I took a picture of this.

Ammunition: 460 rounds expended

–2nd Lt. Ralph J. Hofer

A nice photo of Lt. Ralph Hofer's *Salem Representative*. Hofer not only ran up a big aerial kill score, he destroyed another 14 enemy aircraft on the ground. Hofer's fate was not determined for many years. It was only recently learned that he was shot down and killed in Yugoslavia. *USAAF*

✪Maj. Gerald W. Johnson
16.5 Victories

Maj. Gerald Johnson with his crew chief. Johnson not only was a crack shot, but he had eyes that could see the enemy long before others did. Johnson went on to become a lieutenant general in the U.S. Air Force.

Gerald Walter Johnson was born on July 10, 1919, in Owenton, Kentucky.

Johnson left college to enter the U.S. Army Air Corps as an aviation cadet in September 1941. He received his wings and commission on April 29, 1942, at Ellington Field, Texas. Shortly after graduation he joined the 56th Fighter Group, which was the first unit to fly the P-47 Thunderbolt. Johnson was one of the first successful combat pilots in the group. He transferred to the 356th Fighter Group in November 1943 but returned to the 56th Group in February 1944 as a major and commander of the 63rd Fighter Squadron. Johnson met the same fate as many strafers on March 27, 1944, when he was hit strafing a train. He was taken prisoner and spent the rest of the war in a German stalag luft.

Johnson remained in the Air Force after the war and was promoted to lieutenant colonel in October 1945. He commanded two fighter wings and was promoted to colonel in December 1951. Entering Strategic Air Command in 1956, he commanded the first U-2 unit and then commanded a bomb wing. During the war in Vietnam, as a major general, Johnson commanded the B-52 units operating out of Guam. Promoted to lieutenant general in September 1971, he became the Air Force Inspector General before his retirement in September 1974.

For several years following his retirement, Johnson worked in Saudi Arabia and helped in the organization of the Saudi Air Force.

Johnson now lives in retirement in Sarasota, Florida.

Decorations: Distinguished Service Cross, Distinguished Flying Cross with 4 Oak Leaf Clusters, Bronze Star Medal, and Air Medal with 3 Oak Leaf Clusters.

Assigned aircraft in World War II:
P-47D 42-7877 HV-D *In The Mood*
P-47D 42-75232 UN-Z

```
TYPE OF MISSION:Combat
DATE:17 August 1943
UNIT:61st Fighter Squadron,56th Fighter Group
TIME:1620 hours to 1645 hours
LOCATION OF ACTION:One Me 110 north of Leige, one
Me 109 near Hasselt, one Me 109 near Diest
WEATHER:Ceiling unlimited, visibility slightly hazy
TYPE OF ENEMY AIRCRAFT ENCOUNTERED:Me 110, Me 109
CLAIM:One Me 110 destroyed, two Me 109s destroyed
```

I was leading Keyworth Red flight in the first section of our squadron. We made landfall in over Walcherien Island at 1555 hours at 20,000 feet. We proceeded on course at this altitude to just northeast of Antwerp, where we pulled up to about 22,000 feet and dropped belly tanks. Shortly after this White flight, led by Major Gabreski, made an attack on two Me 109s coming in from the rear. We followed him in the attack, and shortly after this attack he and his wingman returned because of fuel shortage. Since his number-three man had returned sooner because he couldn't release his belly tank, Red flight was all that was left of the first section, so we pulled up to join the second section.

When we reached the bombers, we crossed over the top to take a position on the left side of the last box. As we came out of the left side north of Liege about 25,000 feet, I saw a twin-engine plane almost solid white, or very light gray, flying across the front B–17s in the last box at about 20 degrees to their course. He was flying at about their speed and about 1,000 feet above them. I immediately rolled over and went down on him from dead astern and about 30-degrees angle. At 150 yards I opened fire and could see strikes all through the center of the plane. After about a two-second burst he exploded with a flame about 40 feet in diameter and little pieces seemed to just hang in the air, burning. It is my opinion from his position and action that he was preparing to drop bombs on the B–17s and that my bullets exploded his bombs, because I don't believe anything else could have caused such a tremendous explosion.

We pulled up toward the sun to about 23,000 feet, and upon leveling out saw a single Me 109 going in head-on to the bombers. We came down on him at a steep angle and opened fire at about 200 yards. I could see hits and flashes on the fuselage and wing roots. At this point he started to turn left and a full burst seemed to hit between the cockpit and engine. There was a large flash of flame and smoke, and he started to go down in a slow spiral. As I pulled back up in a climbing turn I saw the pilot bail out, and the chute opened immediately.

We pulled back up to about 1,000 feet above the bombers and to their left. We were approaching the rear of the front box when I saw another single Me 109 coming in from 10 o'clock to the bombers. I couldn't get within range until he broke away from the bombers. I then easily closed to 100 yards without being seen by the enemy aircraft. I fired about a three-second burst, seeing strikes all over the fuselage, and smoke and flame coming out. Without any evasive action he slowly rolled over to the left and went straight down. As I pulled up in a tight climbing turn, I saw the Me 109 hit the ground in a cloud of smoke. I then found that I was by myself (my number-two man and second element had chased two Me 109s off my tail during the last attack). I started for the coast at 17,000 feet. As I neared Antwerp, two Me 109s came up behind me and out to the side but when I turned into them they broke down toward Antwerp. I then proceeded home without further incident.

I attribute the success of this flight or this mission to the splendid cooperation of my wingman, Lieutenant Foster, and my second element, Lieutenant Conger and Lieutenant R. S. Johnson. I claim one Me 110 destroyed and two Me 109s destroyed.

—Capt. Gerald W. Johnson

```
TYPE OF MISSION: Combat
DATE: 10 October 1943
UNIT: 61st Fighter Squadron, 56th Fighter Group
TIME: 1535 hours
LOCATION OF ACTION: North of Munster
WEATHER: CAVU
TYPE OF ENEMY AIRCRAFT ENCOUNTERED: Me 110,
Me 210
CLAIM: One Me 110 destroyed, one Me 210 destroyed
```

I was leading Blue flight in Keyworth Squadron. We crossed the coast going north of the Hague at 25,000 feet and continued on course, picking up the bombers north of Munster at 28,000 feet. As we turned left to take our position on the bombers, I saw 12 to 15 enemy aircraft to the rear of the second box and slightly above them, about 27,000 feet. I saw an Me 110 starting an attack from about four o'clock on a bomber that had fallen back somewhat from the main formation. I called to attack and started down. As I neared the Me 110, I could see large bulges under each wing just outside the engines, which were probably rocket guns. I opened fire at about 300 yards and saw strikes on the fuselage and starboard engine, which started smoking. By this time we were within 200 yards of the B–17s, and the enemy aircraft went under the B–17 very close.

Since I was attacking from slightly above, I had to pull up hard to miss the Fort and went over the top. I then half-rolled and came out on the tail of the Me 110 again. At about 250 yards I opened fire and the port engine started burning. There were strikes near the cockpit and along the fuselage. Then pieces started flying off around the tail, and the enemy aircraft fell off to the left in a spin. I then pulled up in a tight left turn, and the last I saw of the enemy aircraft, it was still spinning down with the left engine and wing burning and the right engine pouring out black smoke. I couldn't observe it any longer, since an FW

190 dived past my nose so close I had to break down to avoid hitting him. I then turned back toward the bombers and there was an Me -210 slightly below me headed toward the bombers from eight o'clock. I started after it and opened fire at about 250 yards. There were strikes on the fuselage and right engine, but since I was closing fast I had to pull up and come down in another attack. On the second attack there were hits all over the fuselage and wings, and the right engine started burning. The rear guns fired at me through the first attack and partway through the second and then stopped firing. The Me 210 then started down in a shallow dive to the left and I made another attack. This time the left engine started burning and pieces were flying off. When I pulled up from this attack, one person bailed out and the enemy aircraft continued going down, burning. We then pulled back up to our position on the left side of the bombers and escorted them to the coast without seeing any more enemy aircraft. I claim one Me 110 destroyed and one Me 210 destroyed.

–Capt. Gerald W. Johnson

✪Capt. Robert S. Johnson

27 Victories

Capt. Robert "Bob" Johnson, 27-victory ace of the 56th Fighter Group, with one of his first P-47s, *Half-Pint. USAAF*

Robert Samuel Johnson was born in Lawton, Oklahoma, on February 24, 1920. After graduating from Cameron Junior College in 1941, he entered the U. S. Army Air Corps and was graduated a pilot from Kelly Field, Texas, on July 3, 1942. He was assigned to the 56th Fighter Group, 61st Fighter Squadron, with which he became an outstanding fighter ace with 27 confirmed aerial victories.

Johnson had to overcome a serious challenge on one of his first missions when his Thunderbolt was damaged and he fell victim to a German pilot, who found it impossible to shoot the P-47 down. Johnson repaid the compliment by destroying 27 Luftwaffe aircraft, all fighters! Johnson left the Air Force following World War II and was a long-time employee of the firm in whose aircraft he had excelled, Republic Aircraft Corporation. Johnson stayed in the Air Force Reserve and was promoted to lieutenant colonel before his retirement. Bob Johnson passed away at his home in South Carolina on December 27, 1998.

Decorations: Distinguished Service Cross, Silver Star, Distinguished Flying Cross with 7 Oak Leaf Clusters, Air Medal with 3 Oak Leaf Clusters, Purple Heart, and British Distinguished Flying Cross.

Known assigned aircraft in World War II:

P-47, *Half Pint*

P-47C 41-6235 HV-P, *All Hell*

P-47D 42-8461 HV-P, *Lucky*

P-47D 42-76234 HV-O, *Double Lucky*

P-47D 42-25512 HV-Q, *Penrod & Sam*

```
TYPE OF MISSION:Combat
DATE:8 March 1944
UNIT:61st Fighter Squadron,56th Fighter Group
TIME:1315 hours
LOCATION OF ACTION:Northeast of Steinhuder Lake
WEATHER:Good
TYPE OF ENEMY AIRCRAFT ENCOUNTERED:Me 109
CLAIM:Two Me 109s destroyed
```

I was leading Halstead Red Flight at 23,000 feet, just about five miles northeast of Steinhuder Lake at 12 o'clock to our box of bombers. I saw 3 enemy aircraft attacking a single Fort, and I saw some parachutes. I attacked and ended up chasing two of them. I chased them for some time, gaining rapidly. I could see their black smoke pour out as they gave full boost. I had 45 inches of mercury and still gained rapidly. I gave a short burst at 500 yards and missed. I saw the black smoke stop suddenly so I chopped my throttle. He made a tight turn right so I pulled up and right and sliced back on his tail. He poured full boost again, and I opened fire at 400 to 500 yards. I finally got a good burst at him at 3,000-feet altitude and overran him. I pulled up to look for him and saw the fire and the smoke as he hit the ground.

I pulled up, and right under me there was an airdrome with at least 25 or 30 planes on it, He 111s and other types. About this time, six to eight P-47s and maybe a few e/a came down on the drome. I went back to 10,000 or 11,000 feet and saw a P-47 with an FW 190 on his tail about 2,000 or 3,000 feet. I called him and told him to climb and turn. The FW followed him for two turns and broke away, and I started down on him. We picked this P-47 up and brought him with us. As we were climbing, another Me 109 jumped my number two and number three. I yelled, "Break left!" As they broke left, the Me 109 turned right and I made a head-on attack, seeing a few strikes. I got on his tail and fired again, going straight down. He was smoking and I last saw him going straight down, well under 2,000 feet and doing well over 450 miles per hour. I didn't have time to see him hit or what happened to him, as we had to break again. This was just north of Steinhuder Lake. I had excellent teamwork on my flight. I claim two Me 109s destroyed.

—*1st Lt. Robert S. Johnson*

```
o                                                              o
   TYPE OF MISSION:Combat
   DATE:9 April 1944
   UNIT:61st Fighter Squadron,56th Fighter Group
   TIME:1130 hours
   LOCATION OF ACTION:Northwest of Keil, over water
   WEATHER:Hazy but good
   TYPE OF ENEMY AIRCRAFT ENCOUNTERED:FW 190
   CLAIM:One 190 destroyed
o                                                              o
```

I was flying Keyworth Red Leader. My number two and number four aborted, but at landfall Lieutenant Hamilton, my number three, and I went on. I could not release my belly tanks but decided to go on as we only had 15 or 20 minutes to go. Someone called in contrails at three o'clock to the bombers, 10 to 15 miles away. The bombers were 18,000 or 19,000 feet. Everyone started after the contrails, myself included. We passed over the bombers, having been on the left side, and climbed to 23,000. I looked back and saw 20-millimeters flashing around the lower lead box of bombers. Lieutenant Hamilton and I rolled to the left and attacked the 15 FW 190s. They had dived down and were coming up from the rear and beneath the Libs. We got on their tail and began tangling. Some rolled to the deck. I fired a short burst at one and broke into two FW 190s on my tail. These two went on to get on Lieutenant Hamilton's tail, so I tangled with two more FWs. I got rid of these two and began to look for more targets. I saw Lieutenant Hamilton on the water northwest of Kiel, turning with two FWs on his tail. One FW would turn with him and the other would pull out and make a head-on pass. He called for help and I told him to keep turning and hold out; that I was coming as fast as I could. I still had the belly tank on and was at 18,000 feet. I went down but was going so fast I couldn't get on one of them. I fired at one making head-on passes to scare him off and they broke off Lieutenant Hamilton's tail. Lieutenant Hamilton hit the one making head-on passes, and he burned and went to sea 1,000 feet below. I watched it as Lieutenant Hamilton got on the other. Then the other FW got on me. I gave throttle and outclimbed the FW 190 in a spiral to the left. He dropped his nose as he stalled and I rolled over and got on his tail. Lieutenant Hamilton had also hit the one in the left wing tip. The FW would break into me every time I tried to line up on him. I fired several times at him, seeing strikes twice. He turned inland and I got on his tail again, firing and hitting him. He bailed out. Most of the firing was deflection, and I'd say about 400 to 500 yards. I confirm one FW 190 destroyed by Lieutenant Hamilton plus one FW 190 damaged by him. I claim one FW 190 destroyed.

–Capt. Robert S. Johnson

Capt. Robert Johnson and another of his Thunderbolts, *Lucky*. He really realized how lucky he was when an FW 190 failed to down him when he was helpless. *USAAF*

```
TYPE OF MISSION:Combat
DATE:8 May 1944
UNIT:62st Fighter Squadron
TIME:1000 hours
LOCATION OF ACTION:Vicinity between Brunswick and
Hanover
WEATHER:Hazy; broken low clouds
TYPE OF ENEMY AIRCRAFT ENCOUNTERED:Me 109, FW 190
CLAIM:One ME 109, one FW 190 destroyed
```

I was flying Platform Leader on a bomber escort mission near Brunswick, Germany. We had swept the area south of Brunswick and were going north. When we were somewhere north of Brunswick, I think, maybe a little west of there, I looked back and saw the line of bombers at seven o'clock to me. One was going down burning. They were 10 miles south of us. I called it in, and we went back to look them over. On the way, I saw an Me 109 diving under me at three o'clock to me. I rolled over and went after him. I caught him easily and he tried to turn with me. I turned inside him at about 11,000 feet and fired a fairly close range. We had started after him at 19,000 feet. I couldn't see if I had him then, because he was under my nose. He thought I turned inside of him, so he straightened out to dive away. Then I had him; I fired at 400 yards. We were both aileron rolling. I pulled up as his wing came off and the ship hit the ground. The pilot did not get out.

We pulled up going south to an area slightly east of Hanover that looked like it had plenty of business. My number three called in two FW 190s diving and going south. I told him to go get them. I saw them then and told him not to go under the clouds, but he went on, probably not hearing me. I told him I would pick them up on the other side of the cloud, as they were low, scattered clouds, tops 3,000 to 4,000 feet. We had started after them at 12,000 to 13,000 feet. They came out of the clouds circling left and I was turning right. When the P-47 came out, instead of him chasing the two FWs, four FWs were chasing him. I told the P-47 to climb and turn if he couldn't get in the clouds. He turned and climbed and was getting away from them and also getting them up so that we could help him. As I was going in the opposite direction, I kept making head-on passes at them, getting the last two off and getting hits on the nose of the second one. I saw only a few strikes on the FW head-on, and he rolled over with a little smoke trailing as I pulled up. I didn't watch him, as I was still trying to get the last FW off. Then the P-47, who later turned out to be my number-four man and who had lost his leader, seemed to tire of the turn and climb, and straightened out a second. At the time, I saw strikes on the left side of the P-47's engine, and the pilot bailed out. The FW 190 that I had hit in the engine was seen to smoke, then catch on fire and explode by four or five of my fellow pilots there with me. The pilot was not seen to get out. I claim one Me and one FW 190 destroyed.

–Capt. Robert S. Johnson

```
TYPE OF MISSION:Combat
DATE:31 December 1943
UNIT:61st Fighter Squadron,56th Fighter Group
TIME:1400 hours
LOCATION OF ACTION:North of St. Gilles
WEATHER:Good visibility, low scattered clouds, 5/10
coverage top at 4,000 feet
TYPE OF ENEMY AIRCRAFT ENCOUNTERED:FW 190
CLAIM:Two FW 190s destroyed
```

I was flying Keyworth Yellow Leader. I was circling the front two boxes of bombers when one of the other flights called bandits in below at six o'clock. I was then at 19,000 feet, going north with the bombers. I rolled over on my back and saw two FW 190s directly underneath at about 14,000 feet, attacking the low box of bombers head-on. I looked behind them and counted four more in string below them. I aileron-rolled down and took the last one. I pulled away when they got near the bombers. I saw one direct hit on one of the bombers as the FWs flew through them.

On the wing of his final P-47, *Penrod and Sam*, Capt. Robert Johnson leans on the scoreboard, which shows 25 kills. *USAAF*

I swung left with my flight and picked them up as they dived from the rear of the bombers to the left. One of the bandits turned right and up. As I went in after the other five, my number three and number four kept this one off our tails. They were leaving us, so I added throttle and gained quickly. Again I picked the last one. It looked like they were going into the clouds, so I opened fire at about 800 or 900 yards. I missed the first short burst and raised my sights. I saw strikes and pieces came off. He split-essed and dived into the ground from about 4,000 feet.

I picked the number-four FW 190 next, because the fifth one dived immediately into the clouds. I fired at about the same range and saw an explosion and pieces came off. He dropped his left wing and went straight into the ground.

By this time the leader pulled up to the left and I found out I only had one man with me. I banked right to see if my tail was clear and having much more speed than they, I zoomed for the leader. He immediately rolled to the right and the others followed him. They all went to the deck and under the clouds. I made a zoom climb and leveled out about 14,000 feet at 250 miles per hour. I then pulled into a tight left turn and saw an Me 109 going into the sun at about 16,000 feet on our tails. I gave it the throttle and headed into him. Apparently he was in a hurry, for he kept going due east as if he never saw us. We then rejoined the bombers and headed home. I never saw the pilots bail out. I claim two FW 190s destroyed.

—1st Lt. Robert S. Johnson

✪Maj. Walker M. Mahurin
20.25 Victories

Another top ace of the 56th Fighter Group was Capt. Walker "Bud" Mahurin, with 20.25 victories. Downed by a gunner in a German bomber, Mahurin evaded capture and got back to England. *USAAF*

Walker Melville Mahurin was born on December 5, 1918, in Ann Arbor, Michigan.

Mahurin entered the U.S. Army Air Corps in 1941. He graduated from flight training on April 29, 1942. He joined the 56th Fighter Group's 63rd Fighter Squadron and became one of its top scorers in the P-47. Mahurin was a major when he was shot down by the gunner of a Dornier Do 217 on March 2, 1944. He was rescued by the French underground and returned to

England. Mahurin was not allowed to fly further combat in Europe, so he was returned to the United States.

Mahurin went to the Southwest Pacific as CO of the Third Air Commando Squadron in late 1944. He was credited with one victory with that unit before he was shot down on January 14, 1945, and returned to the United States.

Mahurin went back to war in 1952 with the 51st Fighter Interceptor Wing in Korea, where he was credited with the destruction of 3 1/2 MiG 15s. Colonel Mahurin then took over as CO of the Fourth Fighter Interceptor Wing in March 1952, but was shot down and became a prisoner of war on May 13, 1952.

Mahurin left the Air Force in 1956 but continued actively in the Air Force Reserve until his retirement.

Decorations: (World War II): Distinguished Service Cross, Silver Star, Distinguished Flying Cross with 5 Oak Leaf Clusters, and Air Medal with 5 Oak Leaf Clusters; (Korea): Distinguished Flying Cross. Air Medal, and Purple Heart.

Assigned aircraft in World War II:

P-47C 41-6334 UN-M

P-47D 42-8487 UN-M, *Spirit of Atlantic City New Jersey*

```
TYPE OF MISSION: Combat
DATE: 4 october 1943
UNIT: 63rd Fighter Squadron, 56th Fighter Group
TIME: 1132-1140 hours
LOCATION OF ACTION: East of Duren
WEATHER: Clear
TYPE OF ENEMY AIRCRAFT ENCOUNTERED: Me 110
CLAIM: Three Me 110s destroyed
```

I was leading Postgate Blue Section with a flight composed of Flight Officer Cavallo, Lieutenant Vogt, and Lieutenant Wilson. Our penetration was uneventful, but as we made a left turn from the south at about 27,000 feet to cover the last bunch of bombers east of Duren, my number three (Lieutenant Vogt) called to report a bandit in front, attacking bombers. I was unable to see it, so I told him to bounce and I would cover him.

As we went down, I sighted an Me 110 and notified Lieutenant Vogt that I was flying at about 20,000 feet parallel to the bombers. I throttled back and bounced down sun on it and opened fire at 300 yards from the rear. I observed several strikes on both engines and fuselage. I was closing so fast that I overran it and passed by about 20 feet away from it. At the time the right engine was on fire. I broke to the left and started to climb up. When I looked back, I could see the Me 110 flaming and going straight in.

As I pulled back up, several 110s passed in front and slightly above me. I took several deflection shots but saw no hits.

When I had gained about 2,000 feet, I saw another Me 110 flying away from the bombers at right angles to them. I again throttled back and bounced. When I opened fire from about 300 yards, I saw a couple of strikes. The enemy aircraft flipped over on its back, and I did the same. I fired at it upside down, and again saw a few strikes. The Me 110 then started to head straight down. I followed and saw more strikes on it while we were both headed straight down. I broke off at about 18,000 feet and started to climb up. By this time I had lost my wingman and was alone. I did not observe what happened to this bandit.

I climbed back to about 20,000 feet when I again sighted an Me 110 in a dive heading directly away from the bombers. He looked like he was going home. I started down on him and when I got to about 300 yards, I again opened fire from his rear. This time I saw many strikes around the engines and the fuselage. I closed fast and before I pulled up I went past the bandit. I pulled up and started to climb. When I looked back I saw the Me 110 with the right engine flaming and pieces falling off. As the flames extended along the fuselage, I saw parachutes start to open be-hind it. By this time I was near Cologne at about 17,000 feet. I took the course out while climbing. After about 20 minutes, I caught up with the bombers and shortly after joined up with a P-47 from another squadron. We covered the bombers uneventfully, and when the group commander called to tell us to leave, we returned to base. I claim three Me 110s destroyed.

–Capt. Walker M. Mahurin

```
TYPE OF MISSION: Combat
DATE: 3 November 1943
UNIT: 63rd Fighter Squadron, 56th Fighter Group
TIME: 1333-1335; 1350 hours
LOCATION OF ACTION: North of Esens; north of Juist
WEATHER: 8/10 cloud at 17,000 feet
TYPE OF ENEMY AIRCRAFT ENCOUNTERED: Me 109, Me 110
CLAIM: One Me 109, one Me 110 destroyed
```

I was leading Postgate Blue flight (Captain Mahurin, Lieutenant Wisniewski, Lieutenant O'Connor, and Lieutenant Windmayer) and flying at about 27,000 feet when we first sighted the Forts over Esens. As we approached the last box of Forts I noticed P-38s all over the sky, most of them on the left side of the bomber formations. We were coming in on the left side of the bombers and about 1 mile away from them when I first saw (at about 1331 hours) four P-38s weaving along the side of the Forts with an Me 109 trailing them. The 109 was weaving behind the P-38s, trying to get in position to fire. All this was taking place on the left side of our formation. I peeled down to attack and began to chase the Me 109, flying directly behind him. He was taking evasive action but evidently he did not see us because he did no violent work whatsoever. I waited until I had closed to about 400 yards and then opened fire. I observed many

When Capt. Mahurin could not go back to combat in Europe, he went to the Southwest Pacific, where he scored one victory with the Third Air Commandos. *USAAF*

hits on his wings and fuselage, and when I had ceased fire he was smoking. I passed alongside him and pulled up to the left. The Me 109 started a left turn and headed for clouds about 5,000 feet below. At this time my element leader had positioned himself for an attack. I circled and came into position just behind my element leader (Lieutenant O'Connor), off to his right as he began to fire. I fired a couple of bursts too. This time there were many hits all over the Me 109. Pieces flew off in all directions. As we peeled away from the 109, my wingman from underneath and I from above, I saw it burst into flames and roll over onto its back. The pilot bailed out. The Me 109 then went on down, burning fiercely. This combat began about 27,000 feet and ended at 18,000 feet, and occurred at about 1333 to 1335 hours.

I broke away to the right and again set course trying to catch up with the bombers. My wingman (Lieutenant Wisniewski) and I headed west for several minutes until we sighted a large box of

B-24s. As we came up on them I did an orbit right, thinking there were enemy aircraft on my tail. This put us in a position to the rear of the B-24s and on the same level. At about 1350 hours I spied another enemy aircraft making attacks with rockets at the rear of the last bunch of bombers. We started after it, heading almost due north. It proved to be an Me 110. When we reached it, it had started after the left-hand lower bunch of B-24s. I came up directly astern of it and opened fire at about 400 yards. Again I saw many hits in both engines and the fuselage about 20 feet away from the enemy aircraft, and just as I looked into its cockpit my wingman opened fire. At that time both the rear gunner and the pilot were looking at me. The rear gunner twisted around, grabbed his gun, and started to aim just as my wingman's bullets hit the enemy aircraft. His shots hit the left wing and the rear gunner at the same time. I peeled up and around and started to deliver a second attack. By this time the enemy aircraft was smoking from both engines and was heading for the clouds in a southerly direction. I opened fire from about 400 yards, closing to point-blank. This time I saw a mess of flashes. The enemy aircraft belched black smoke, and my ship was covered with oil from the Jerry. As I broke up and away, I noticed the right engine was in flames from the prop spinner back.

The Me 110 went over on its back and disappeared into the clouds. We assumed a two-man formation and returned to our base uneventfully. I believe the reason I had to make two passes at the enemy aircraft was that three of my guns had malfunctioned and not fired.

If there is any question about the awarding of the first Me 109, I would like to disavow claim to it. I believe that although I damaged it enough to bring it down, Lieutenant O'Connor had a much more devastating effect on it than I did. My claims are thus: Upon the board's decision I will claim one Me 109 destroyed and one Me 110 destroyed. However, if the claim is to be split into half and half, I would like to claim a probable on the Me 109.

—Capt. Walker M. Mahurin

```
TYPE OF MISSION: Combat
DATE: 8 March 1944
UNIT: 63rd Fighter Squadron, 56th Fighter Group
TIME: 1320 hours
LOCATION OF ACTION: Wesendorf Airdrome
WEATHER: Clear, visibility good
TYPE OF ENEMY AIRCRAFT ENCOUNTERED: FW 190,
Ju 88
CLAIM: Two FW 190s, one Ju 88 destroyed
```

I was leading North Grove Squadron with a flight consisting of Captain Mahurin, and Lieutenants LaFlam, Smith, and Matthews. We were designated by the B Group leader to take the left side of the bombers on the second division. The group made landfall and met the big friends at the appointed time and place.

We were at 26,000 feet on the furthest bunch of bombers to the north, where our escort was uneventful until we reached the vicinity of Dummer Lake. Suddenly A Group, ahead of us on the first division, reported bandits coming in for an attack. Our group immediately started up toward the front box, but we were disappointed to find that we could not see any bandits. However, we did spot Ashland, the group leader way off in front of us, circle to the right and start down. Still, when we reached the spot we were unable to sight any Jerrys. At this time it was time for recall, but we were reluctant to start out without firing, especially with all the firing going on around us.

I looked over the side of my ship at an airdrome, which I think was Wesendorf, to see one FW 190 circling the field to the left. The FW 190 was painted gray, and since it was circling over

some forests it was easily spotted. I called the flight and we immediately started down to attack. Because of the difference in altitude,
I was slow in lining the Jerry up and when I got within shooting
distance, he had completed one lap of his circuit and was plenty
aware of our presence. He passed down the runway from west to
east and started straight off at tree-top level. I dropped down behind
him and began to fire. At first, my shooting was rotten, as usual,
and I missed. Finally I got close enough to hit him, noticing several
hits on his fuselage, and it disappeared into the trees. I pulled up to
make another pass at him but he had gone into the trees and
crashed. I claim this FW 190 destroyed.

As we pulled up from this attack, we started to climb up while
heading west. We again passed directly over the same airdrome.
This time we spotted an Me 110, which had taken off and made a
90-degree turn into the traffic pattern. I immediately made a left
turn and started after it. Because I was considerably above him, by
the time I got down to him I was going too fast and firing at too
great an angle to hit him. I passed right over this aircraft and noticed the occupants were looking at me. When I turned around to
make another pass, I saw my number-three man (Lieutenant
Smith) come in behind and hit it severely. When he broke off, the
Me 110 did one more left turn and bellied into a field. It then slid
into a forest and spread falling timber like matchsticks. I will verify
Lieutenant Smith's claim for this Me 110 destroyed.

When the flight broke away from this attack, we passed directly
over the hangar line of the airdrome at 600 feet. While doing so I
noticed many single- and twin-engined aircraft on the ground.
Among them there was one Mustang, several Spitfires, what I believed to be a couple of DC-3s, and many He 111s and Me 110s.
At the same time I saw a Ju 88 that had just taken off. I pulled up
and went down on it. Again I closed very fast. This time I fired and
hit the Ju 88 quite hard. I estimate the range from 200 yards to

point-blank. When it broke up I passed over the nose of this ship. I looked into the cockpit and saw at least four men in the ship. The right engine caught on fire, the ship let down and exploded in a field a short distance from the airdrome. I claim this enemy aircraft destroyed.

For the fourth and last time we again went over the same airdrome. By this time we had reached around 6,000 feet. We saw another gray FW 190 circling the field for a landing. Again we bounced. By this time, everyone in the vicinity of the airdrome was aware of our presence. The pilot of the 190 saw us coming and started off in a southerly direction right on the tree tops. I put on the water and began to close on him. I fired and fired but could observe no hits because my windshield was covered with oil. The Jerry would beetle along the tree tops, and whenever he would come to a field he would drop down on the field again, pulling up to go over the trees. Finally he pulled up to avoid some high-tension wires and I was able to get in a good burst.

By this time the FW 190 was smoking badly. I was able to depress my guns enough to hit him. Prior to this time, I could not depress my guns because in doing so I would go into the trees. When I had expended all my ammunition, I pulled up and broke off the attack. I looked back to see the Jerry start a left turn. However, my number four saw him continue to roll, go over on his back, and plow into a forest. I am claiming this enemy aircraft destroyed.

We broke off this attack and climbed back to 16,000 feet while setting course. The flight assumed a line-abreast formation and we reached home uneventfully. I claim two FW 190s destroyed and one Ju 88 destroyed.

–Capt. Walker M. Mahurin

✪Lt. Col. John C. Meyer
24 Victories

Then-Maj. John C. Meyer when he was flying *Lambie,* his P-47 Thunderbolt, with the 487th Fighter Squadron. *USAAF*

John Charles Meyer was born on April 3, 1919, in Brooklyn, New York.

Meyer attended Dartmouth College until 1939 when he entered the U.S. Army Air Corps. He graduated from flight training on July 26, 1940, at Kelly Field, Texas. After serving as a flight instructor, he was based in Iceland for a year.

Shortly thereafter he was assigned to the 487th Fighter Squadron of the 352nd Fighter Group. Meyer remained in command of this squadron until November 20, 1944, departing as a lieutenant colonel. He obtained 3 victories in P-47s and the other 21 flying P-51 Mustangs.

Meyer returned to Dartmouth following the war and obtained his degree.

Shortly after the outbreak of the conflict in Korea, Meyer, then commanding the Fourth Fighter Group, took his F-86s to Korea, where he flew 31 combat missions and was credited with the destruction of two MiG 15s.

In the ensuing years Meyer joined Strategic Air Command and became its commander in 1972. Following this assignment and his promotion to general, he became vice chief of staff of the Air Force. Meyer retired from the Air Force in August 1974.

Decorations: (World War II): Distinguished Service Cross with 2 Oak Leaf Clusters, Silver Star with Oak Leaf Cluster, Distinguished Flying Cross with 6 Oak Leaf Clusters, Air Medal with 14 Oak Leaf Clusters, and Purple Heart; (Korea): Legion of Merit.

Assigned aircraft in World War II:

P-47D 42-8529 HO-M, *Lambie*

P-51B 42-106471 HO-M, *Lambie II*

P-51D 44-14151 HO-M, *Petie 2nd*

P-51D 44-15041 HO-M, *Petie 3rd*

```
TYPE OF MISSION:Combat
DATE:12 May 1944
UNIT:487th Fighter Squadron
TIME:1235 hours
LOCATION OF ACTION:10 miles southwest of Frankfurt
WEATHER:Vis 2 miles
TYPE OF ENEMY AIRCRAFT ENCOUNTERED:Me 109, He 177,
and unidentified twin-engine aircraft
CLAIM:One Me 109, one He 177 destroyed
```

At the rendezvous with the first box of bombers, just northwest of Frankfurt, we saw a combat wing of B-17s well south of course—about 20 miles. There were several explosions among these bombers and no flak. I led a section toward them, and as we approached, we saw 20 to 25 parachutes floating below at various altitudes. We then saw 15-plus 109s and FW 190s headed toward the bombers. We started to attack but lost them in haze against the ground. We spied another group of 15-plus aircraft that we believed to be enemy, which headed for the deck when we started for them. We again lost them in the thick haze. We were still proceeding toward the bomber box, when about 10-plus Me 109s crossed directly over us at 22,000 feet and started turning in behind us. As we turned into them they headed for the deck again, and then disappeared in the haze—all but one, which I followed. I caught him at 5,000 feet, firing a short burst at 200 yards and 10 degrees deflection. The 109 caught fire and crashed into an airdrome after the pilot had successfully bailed out.

Lt. Col. Meyer, CO of the 487th Fighter Squadron, points out something to his crew chief. This aircraft is *Petie 3rd*. Note the 487th Squadron insignia on the fuselage. *USAAF*

This airdrome had 10-plus He 177s and 20-plus other various aircraft for various types, mostly Twin-Engined. I attacked one of the He 177s, and it caught fire, burning profusely as I left. As I pulled up, I   observed an Me 109, firing on my tail at 250 yards.

He was painted robin egg blue on the bottom and sides, and either black or dark brown on top. In about a turn and a half, I was on his tail. Then he dropped some flaps, unlike other Huns, who in similar situations have broken for the deck and set themselves up, and I was unable to get sufficient deflection. This Jerry continued his tight turn and seemed very willing to continue the fight. I tried dropping 10 degrees, and then 20, of flaps and although this helped momentarily to decrease the radius of turn, my airspeed dropped off so much that nothing was gained by this. At this time I was receiving ground fire from the field directly below, this combat taking place at about 3,000 feet. Just then another 109 joined in the fight, climbing above and dropping down behind me. As he lost ground, climbing up again and attacking, I completed the next orbit. I then broke for the deck, flying as low as possible, and headed south into the sun, using valleys and hills for evasion. The Hun followed me for a while but always out of range. I pulled 67 inches for 30 minutes, and somewhere in that time lost them. I claim one Me 109 destroyed and one He 177 destroyed.

Ammunition: 354 rounds expended, API and Incendiary

–Lt. Col. John C. Meyer

```
TYPE OF MISSION:Combat
DATE:11 September 1944
UNIT:487th Fighter Squadron
TIME:1150 hours
LOCATION OF ACTION:Gottingen, Nordhousen,
Mulhousen, 28,000 feet to deck
WEATHER:5/10 low altocumulus
TYPE OF ENEMY AIRCRAFT ENCOUNTERED:Me 109,
FW 190
CLAIM:Three Me 109s, one FW 190 destroyed
```

While sweeping in the above area en route to rendezvous with bombers, we sighted bomber formations from the preceding task force 50 miles southeast of us pulling contrails. About half the distance between the bombers and ourselves were 30-plus single-engine fighters in three gaggles of 10 each. They were pulling contrails and appeared to be forming up. We headed toward them, and as we got closer they dove out of contrail level in ones and twos. Contrail level was 28,000 feet, a plus. At 29,000 feet, I identified two of them as Me 109s and attacked one as he headed down in a 60-degree dive. The whole squadron then engaged small groups of the enemy aircraft after their original gaggle had been split up. At about 17,000 feet, the Me 109 that I was chasing leveled off, and I closed rapidly. He saw me and started in a steep climbing turn; my first burst was about 20-degrees deflection at 300 yards. I observed a few hits. I closed on him in the climbing turn and at 30-degrees deflection and 200 yards. I got hits on the rear portion of his fuselage, pieces coming off. He did a split-ess, recovered, and turned into me. I had little difficulty in overtaking and in turning inside of him. At 20

Lt. Col. Meyer takes a look at Maj. George Preddy's Distinguished Service Cross. Before war's end, Meyer would have three of them. *USAAF*

degrees and 300 yards, I got good strikes on the wing root and it started to smoke. It rolled over and crashed straight into the deck from 8,000 feet. The pilot seemed inexperienced, as his breaks were conspicuously nonviolent. He was hesitant in all his maneuvers.

After completion of this engagement, I was separated from my squadron. Seeing what appeared to be a dogfight to the northwest, I proceeded to that area at 14,000 feet to discover that it consisted of a gaggle of 15-plus bandits (109s and 190s) at 12,000 to 8,000 feet. They had belly tanks and appeared to be forming up. I approached them from out of the sun and attacked the number two of a pair that were farthest from the mass. I fired at 15-degrees deflection from 300 yards to point-blank range. The enemy aircraft burst into flames. I broke into the sun, cleared my tail, and attacked the element leader, at 300 yards. I got a few strikes on his right wing tip and he broke. As he broke I got strikes in the vicinity of cockpit and wing roots. It rolled over and spiraled down, crashing into the ground. Neither of these pilots appeared to have observed my attacks until they were hit.

I then saw a lone Me 109 emerging from a cloud in the vicinity of the large enemy gaggle. And as I was not yet under attack I attacked the 109. Only my right wing guns were now firing, so I opened at 200 yards and no deflection, closing to point-blank range and 10-degrees deflection. I saw strikes all over the aircraft, and pieces flew off the tail and fuselage. He caught fire on the left wing root. I broke off the attack and headed for the deck and home. Shortly thereafter, two Me 109s attacked me from slightly below and directly astern. I pulled 67 inches for 30 seconds and when I got detonation reduced throttle to 55 inches. I climbed at l,000 feet per minute. The 109s remained about 300 yards astern and always 3,000 or 4,000 feet below. Occasionally they would pull up their noses and fire but would then drop behind. They chased me from the vicinity of Kassel to Bonn, breaking off their attack when I reached the Rhine River. I claim three Me 109s and one FW 190 destroyed.

Ammunition: 587 rounds expended (API)

—Lt. Col. John C. Meyer

```
TYPE OF MISSION: Combat
DATE: 31 December 1944
UNIT: 328th Fighter Squadron, 352nd Fighter Group
TIME: Approx. 1100 hours
LOCATION OF ACTION: Vicinity of Euskirchen, Germany
WEATHER: 10/10 low clouds, tops at 3,000 to 4,000
feet
TYPE OF ENEMY AIRCRAFT ENCOUNTERED: AR 234
CLAIM: One AR 234 destroyed (Air)
```

Leading 328th Fighter Squadron at 12,000 feet on area patrol, we were vectored to Viviers by the controller. Bandits were reported at 4,000 feet. We let down through a hole north of Viviers flying at about 6,000 feet under cloud at 8,000 feet and over cloud tops at 3,000 feet, with cumulus development up to the bottom of the higher cloud layer. Traveling south and just about over Viviers was spotted one enemy jet-propelled aircraft, believed to be an Arado 234 going northeast. The squadron turned in place and Captain Bryan's flight was then at 12 o'clock to me and 6 o'clock to the enemy aircraft. I saw Captain Bryan get some good hits on the starboard engine. Just then I saw another enemy aircraft of the same type pull up underneath Captain Bryan, at 6 o'clock to him. Calling for him to break, I gave chase, firing one burst at 1,500 yards before it pulled up into the overcast. I climbed up through the overcast and spotted the target at 11 o'clock to me and heading 60 degrees. Since I was between the target aircraft and the Rhine, I continued chase. I seemed to be neither gaining nor losing ground, pulling 67 inches and 3,000 rpm. Just west of Bonn, he went back into clouds (top 10,000 ft.) and I went under also, losing sight of him. I continued on this heading and again sighted the enemy aircraft in a port turn at 5,000 feet above 10/1 low clouds, tops. At 3,000–4,000 feet I was able to close and fire two two-second bursts at 700 and 600 yards, 30-degrees deflection. I observed no strikes, but he jettisoned his canopy (or escape hatch). To avoid going into the cloud in a vertical bank, I broke off the attack and momentarily lost sight of the enemy aircraft. A few seconds later, swinging around a small cumulus at the top of the clouds, I saw him headed straight down, going into the overcast at 3,000 feet. Circling the area, I saw another enemy aircraft of the same type headed toward Cologne. I gave chase, firing several bursts at extreme range but observing no hits. Being low on gas, White Two and I turned west, five miles north of a large landing strip east of Euskirchen. There we sighted 12-plus Me 109s with belly tanks or bombs in three flights, one at 5,000 feet and high, one at approximately 10,000 feet. We flew right through the enemy formation head-on and headed direct for base. We did not engage the enemy aircraft, who obviously saw us but did not give chase. I claim one Ar 234 destroyed.

Jet-propelled enemy aircraft was same size and general fuselage as A-26. No canopy bulge on top of fuselage, glass-enclosed nose, fuselage shape generally conforms with that of Arado 234 diagrams, although nose seemed more bulbous, similar to Ju 88. Plan view showed wings swept in similar plan form of Ju 90. Engine nacelles were very close to fuselage. Believe good shot of plan view will appear in combat film.

–Lt. Col. John C. Meyer

✪Maj. Robin Olds
13 Victories

Maj. Robin Olds was a latecomer to the Eighth Air Force, as the 479th Group came in just before D-Day. Although Olds didn't score until August 1944, he wound up with 13 kills: 5 in the P-38 and 8 in the Mustang. *USAAF*

Robin Olds was born on July 14, 1922, in Honolulu, Hawaii. Olds' father was a career Air Service officer and he grew up with aircraft. His father became the commander of the first B-17 group in the 1930s and was one of the real pioneers of the Air Force. Olds attended West Point and graduated with the Class of 1943, already rated as a pilot. He joined the 479th Group and went to England with the group in the spring of 1944. The unit originally flew P-38s, and Olds scored five victories to become an ace in one. He scored another eight victories and was CO of the 434th Fighter Squadron and a major when the war ended.

Following the war he did an exchange tour with the Royal Air Force and returned to lead several fighter units, although, much to his chagrin, he missed combat in Korea.

Colonel Olds led the Eighth Tactical Fighter Wing from Thailand, flying F-4s from September 1966 until September 1967.

During his tour he destroyed four enemy aircraft. He was promoted to brigadier general in 1968 and retired from the Air Force in June 1973.

Decorations: (World War II): Silver Star with Oak Leaf Cluster, Distinguished Flying Cross with Oak Leaf Cluster and Air Medal with 27 Oak Leaf Clusters; (Vietnam) Air Force Cross, Distinguished Service Medal with Oak Leaf Cluster, Silver Star with Oak Leaf Cluster, Distinguished Flying Cross with 2 Oak Leaf Clusters, and Air Medal with 11 Oak Leaf Clusters.

Assigned aircraft in World War II:

P-38J 43-28341 L2-W, *Scat II*

P-51D L2-W, *Scat IV*

```
TYPE OF MISSION:Combat
DATE:14 August 1944
UNIT:434th Fighter Squadron, 479nd Fighter Group
TIME:0700 hours
LOCATION OF ACTION:Vicinity of Montmirail, France
WEATHER:Clear, visibilty 5 to 8 miles in haze
TYPE OF ENEMY AIRCRAFT ENCOUNTERED:FW 190
CLAIM:Two FW 190s destroyed
```

I was flying Newcross Red Two on a Fighter Rhubarb mission under Eighth Fighter Command Field Order 513. In the vicinity of Montmirail, France, I became slightly separated from the rest of the flight on a dive-bombing run. I was alone on the deck headed approximately 330 degrees, when I saw two unidentified aircraft one or two miles away, at one o'clock in a turn heading 70 degrees at an altitude of approximately 200 feet. I cut across below them and pulled up behind and identified them positively as FW 190s. Then I opened fire on the trailing 190 from dead astern at about 400 yards and fired a five- to eight-second burst. I observed many strikes on the left wing and the left side of the fuselage, so I changed point of aim slightly to the right and put a concentrated burst into the fuselage. I observed big pieces flying off the German aircraft, and wisps of flame and heavy black smoke poured out from it. He then went into an uncontrolled half-roll, going down to the right. At this time we were both just above the trees, at an altitude of not over 100 feet.

The second enemy aircraft broke left in a violent evasive skid right on the deck, and I followed. I did not observe the first German hit the ground, because my right wing blanketed it off. I was turning inside the German, so I fired in short bursts at a range of approximately 300 to 200 yards, observing a few strikes. The German did a complete 360-degree turn and pulled out straight and level, still on the deck. Then I fired again, approximately a five-second burst from dead astern, and observed many strikes. Large pieces of the German ship flew off. He then zoomed and I followed, continuing to fire, with still more strikes and pieces occurring. At the top of the zoom, the German pilot parachuted, his chute opening almost at once, so that I had to cock up a wing to keep from hitting him. I saw the second German ship hit the ground and explode. I claim two FW 190s destroyed in the air.

Ammunition expended: 150 rounds 20-millimeter (HEI); 1,200 rounds .50-caliber (API)

—Capt. Robin Olds

```
TYPE OF MISSION: Combat
DATE: 7 April 1945
UNIT: 434th Fighter Squadron, 479th Fighter Group
TIME: 1220-1245 hours
LOCATION OF ACTION: Area between Dummer Lake and
Bremen
WEATHER: 7-9 tenths undercast, top 8,000 feet; haze
layer at 26,000 feet
TYPE OF ENEMY AIRCRAFT ENCOUNTERED: Me 262,
Me 109, FW 190
CLAIM: One Me 109 destroyed, one Me 262 damaged
```

By arrangement with the 355th Group, which was also escorting the first box of B-24s, I positioned my group on the north side of the box. The 355th Group took the south side.

At about 1220 hours we were at 27,000 feet, nine o'clock high to the bombers. Our position was approximately midway between Bremen and Dummer Lake. I noticed contrails popping up over a cirrus bank at nine o'clock to us. This cirrus layer ran east-west. Someone in the squadron called these contrails in about a minute later. We eased over toward them. I left two squadrons very close to the bombers and took only my squadron on this investigation. The contrails cut off; a few seconds later I saw 12 Me 262s diving on the bombers. They were flying good formation, being in three flights of four each, line abreast in flights, flights in trail. At this moment, Nuthouse called in bogies approaching our bomber force from the southwest. The jets were approaching the bombers from nine o'clock high. I split-essed on top of them, stalled, shuttered, and fired. It was a snap shot that achieved no hits. At the end of the split-ess I found myself directly behind the blow jobs and headed for the bombers with them. I ranged and fired at the Me 262 playing tail-end Charlie, but was far out of range. I did see one large puff of black smoke emitted from the jet while I was firing but cannot say whether or not I had got a strike on him. This particular jet went right between two boxes without firing and started a turn to the right, presumably for another pass, when he must have seen two flights of us behind him, for he straightened out and left us far behind. He headed for the B-17 stream to the south.

I turned around and headed back for our bombers, which were not far distant.

As I passed the second box in our force, I saw an Me 109 going in on the bombers. I tacked onto him and followed him right through the box. I couldn't fire until he passed through the box for fear of hitting a bomber myself. The Me 109 fired at one bomber from eight o'clock high in a steep dive. He clobbered the bomber. I cut loose then, being in range, and immediately got strikes; he rolled, I followed, getting a few more strikes, then he bailed out. His airplane went straight in.

I lost a wheel fairing door in my dive after the 109 and from then on could attain no appreciable rate of climb and no sufficient air speed. I met the Me 109 at approximately 1245 hours, at 21,000 feet as the bombers turned to start their bombing run.

Later I tried to climb to some Me 109s several thousand feet above me, but couldn't do any good with my damaged plane. I had to sit there and watch some unidentified P-51s pass me and hit the 109s. Still later, I caught another 109 going in on a box of B-17s. I gave chase, having to go right through P-51s escorting this particular box. The bombers needed no help, for they destroyed the Me 109 before I closed on him. I saw this ship go into the ground and explode. After another futile attempt to get up to a high gaggle of 109s, I headed for home.

The entire action took place between the hours of 1220 and about 1315. The weather was excellent, ground and air visibility being exceptionally good.

I would like to commend the pilots of the group for their good work this day. A close escort, cooperation between squadrons, individual aggressiveness, and overall alertness saved the bomber force from many intended attacks. I claim one Me 109 destroyed and one Me 262 damaged.

Ammunition: 377 rounds expended (.50-caliber API)

—Maj. Robin Olds

⊙Maj. Richard A. Peterson
15.5 Victories

Capt. Richard A. Peterson is shown returning from a combat mission. Peterson was a 15.5-victory ace with the 364th Fighter Squadron, and came back for a second tour with the 357th group. *Kramer*

Richard Allen Peterson was born on February 26, 1923, in Hancock, Minnesota.

Peterson was attending the University of Minnesota when he left to become an aviation cadet in June 1942. He graduated from flight training on March 10, 1943, at Yuma, Arizona. Peterson was assigned to the 364th Fighter Squadron of the 357th Fighter Group and flew two combat tours with this organization. Peterson scored 11.5 of his victories on his first tour.

Peterson left the Air Force at the end of the war and returned to the University of Minnesota to get his degree as an architect, which became his life's profession.

Peterson succumbed to cancer on June 4, 2000.

Decorations: Silver Star, Distinguished Flying Cross with 3 Oak Leaf Clusters, and Air Medal with 10 Oak Leaf Clusters.

Assigned aircraft in World War II:
P-51B 43-6935 C5-T, *Hurry Home Honey*
P-51D 44-13586 C5-T, *Hurry Home Honey*
P-51D 44-14868 C5-T, *Hurry Home Honey*

```
TYPE OF MISSION: Combat
DATE: 1 July 1944
UNIT: 364th Fighter Squadron, 357th Fighter Group
TIME: 2030-2040 hours
LOCATION OF ACTION: East of St. Quentin
WEATHER: Broken clouds at 8,000 feet
TYPE OF ENEMY AIRCRAFT ENCOUNTERED: Me 109
CLAIM: One Me 109 and pilot destroyed
```

I was leading Greenhouse Blue flight and had just shot down an Me 109 when I heard someone calling for help on the R/T. I saw a rat race going on a short distance south of me and went over to join. When I got there, an Me 109 and a P-51 of our group—362nd Squadron—were in a tight Lufbery to the left, neither one gaining on the other. The enemy aircraft had already knocked one P-51 down. The pilot of the Me 109 was really a sharp pilot, and I believe he was gaining on the P-51. He was "walking" his ship around the circle.

I kept making passes at him while the P-51 held him in the Lufbery. I observed strikes on the wings and fuselage. The pilot then flew into the ground and exploded. I claim one Me 109 and pilot destroyed, thanks to the upright guns of a P-51D.

Ammunition: 680 rounds expended

—*Capt. Richard A. Peterson*

```
TYPE OF MISSION: Combat
DATE: 2 November 1944
UNIT: 364th Fighter Squadron, 357th Fighter Group
TIME: 1245 hours
LOCATION OF ACTION: Northwest of Merseburg
WEATHER: 10/10 at 5,000 feet
TYPE OF ENEMY AIRCRAFT ENCOUNTERED: FW 190
CLAIM: One FW 190 destroyed
```

Hurry Home Honey was one of several ships of the same name flown by Capt. Richard Peterson. It was named for the manner in which his wife closed each of her letters to him. *USAAF*

bombers, number-two box, had already made their run. Since our box was pretty well covered with P-51s, I decided to circle until the last box came through. I made a sweep south of the target, where some jets were reported, but to no avail. I came back in time to intercept 20-plus enemy aircraft making a six o'clock pass at approximately the last box. I couldn't get in an effective pass because there were so many from the 352nd Group around. I finally hit the deck and came across a lone FW 190 under the overcast. He saw me and started to climb into it. He no sooner started up than he came back out of it. He turned to the left and I took a three-radii lead from about 250 yards and fired two bursts. I caught him with the second burst—hitting him from the nose to the cockpit. He spun into the ground, firing his guns, and exploded. I claim one FW 190 and pilot destroyed.

Ammunition expended: 450 rounds

—*Capt. Richard A. Peterson*

✪Maj. George E. Preddy Jr.

26.83 Victories

Maj. George Preddy in the cockpit of *Cripes A'Mighty 3rd*. Preddy scored 13.5 victories, including his 6 in one day, in this aircraft. *USAAF*

George E. Preddy Jr. was born on February 5, 1919, in Greensboro, North Carolina.

Preddy joined the U.S. Army Air Corps and graduated from flight training at Craig Field, Alabama, on December 2, 1941. He was sent to the Southwest Pacific to join the 49th Fighter Group. On July 12, 1942, he was involved in a midair collision and, due to his injuries, was sent back to the United States. In December 1942 he joined the 352nd Fighter Group and went to England with the group, flying P-47 Thunderbolts.

Preddy scored three victories in the P-47, but once he got into flying P-51s his score rose rapidly. When he returned to the United

States on leave in August 1944, he had scored 22.83 victories. He returned to the 352nd Group in October 1944 as CO of the 328th Fighter Squadron. He would score another four victories before he was killed by friendly machine gun fire on Christmas Day 1944.

Decorations: Distinguished Service Cross, Silver Star with Oak Leaf Cluster, Distinguished Flying Cross with 8 Oak Leaf Clusters, and Air Medal with 7 Oak Leaf Clusters.

Assigned aircraft in World War II:

P-47D 42-8521 HO-Y

P-47D 42-8500 HO-P, *Cripes A'Mighty*

P-51B 42-106451 HO-P, *Cripes A'Mighty 2nd*

P-51D 44-13321 HO-P, *Cripes A'Mighty 3rd*

P-51D 44-14906 PE-P, *Cripes A'Mighty*

```
TYPE OF MISSION: Combat
DATE: 30 May 1944
UNIT: 487th Fighter Squadron
TIME: 1115-1130 hours
LOCATION OF ACTION: Vicinity of Magdeburg, 25,000
to 5,000 feet
WEATHER: CAVU
TYPE OF ENEMY AIRCRAFT ENCOUNTERED: Me 109
CLAIM: Three Me 109s destroyed
```

As the bombers were approaching the vicinity of Magdeburg, I was leading a section of seven ships giving close support to the rear box, which was quite a way behind the main formation. I noticed 20 to 30 single-engine fighters attacking the front boxes, so we dropped our tanks and headed toward them. We came up behind three Me 109s in a rather tight formation. I opened fire on one from 300 yards and closed to 150. The enemy aircraft burst into flames and went down. I then slipped behind the second 109 and fired from 200 to 100 yards. He started burning and falling apart, and went down spinning. The third enemy aircraft saw us and broke down. I followed him in a steep turn, diving and zooming. I got in many deflection shots, getting hits on the wings and tail section. I ran out of ammo, so my element leader, Lieutenant Whisner, continued the attack, getting in several good hits. At about 7,000 feet, the pilot bailed out. I claim two Me 109s destroyed and one Me 109 destroyed (shared with Lieutenant Whisner)

Ammunition: 352 rounds expended

—Maj. George E. Preddy

```
TYPE OF MISSION: Combat
DATE: 20 June 1944
UNIT: 487th Fighter Squadron
TIME: 0920-0945 hours
LOCATION OF ACTION: East of Bernburg, 28,000 feet
to deck
WEATHER: 2 to 4/10 clouds at 5,000 feet
TYPE OF ENEMY AIRCRAFT ENCOUNTERED: Me 410,
FW 190
CLAIM: One Me 410, one FW 190 destroyed
```

I was group leader and leading a squadron of 12 aircraft supporting the first combat wing of B-17s bombing Magdeburg. Just after the bombers reached the target, I saw 15 Me 410s forming up in the sun at 28,000 feet. We flew out and intercepted them from 1,000 feet above. All enemy aircraft went into a tight Lufbery except one that broke down. I followed him, and after he leveled off at 6,000 feet above a cloud, I fired a short burst and he went into the cloud. I went below and he turned into me going back up through the cloud. I picked him up again on top and back down through he went. After following him through the cloud five or six times, I lost him altogether.

My wingman, Lieutenant Wood, and I started climbing back up and saw an FW 190 slightly above us. He turned down and fired at my number two, and I got a head-on shot at the 190.

After several deflection shots, I got on his tail and got a good long burst into him. The pilot bailed out at 2,000 feet. Again we started climbing and saw an Me 410 above us. I managed to get on his tail and got a few hits before overshooting. Lieutenant Wood pulled in and got a good burst into him, and one of the crew bailed out. The 410 lost a lot of speed and went into the ground and exploded. I claim one FW 190 destroyed and one Me 410 destroyed (shared with Lieutenant Wood).

Ammunition: 1,143 rounds expended

–Maj. George E. Preddy

```
TYPE OF MISSION:Combat
DATE:18 July 1944
UNIT:487th Fighter Squadron
TIME:0900 hours
LOCATION OF ACTION:Northeast of Rostock, 25,000 to
5,000 feet
WEATHER:9/10 cloud, tops at 1,000 feet
TYPE OF ENEMY AIRCRAFT ENCOUNTERED:Me 109, Ju 88
CLAIM:One Me 109, three Ju 88s destroyed; Two Ju 88s
damaged
```

I was leading the squadron on a sweep south of the bombers and heading north to intercept the bombers. Yellow Leader called in bandits at four o'clock low. I made a right turn up sun of the enemy formation, which consisted of a mess of Ju 88s with many Me 109s as top cover. I took my flight of three, Lieutenants Vickery and Greer and myself, to attack the Ju 88s, about 50 in number, while the rest of the squadron dealt with the top cover. As we approached the formation I saw a single Me 109 ahead of me and attacked it from quarter-stern. I opened fire at 400 yards and drove up his tail. The 109 was covered with hits and went down burning and falling apart.

I continued to attack the Ju 88 formation and opened fire on one of them, knocking off many pieces and setting the plane on fire. Lieutenant Greer then called a break to the right, as an Me 109 was pulling up on my tail from below. After we broke, the 109 stalled out and went down. During this maneuver, Lieutenant Greer became separated. Lieutenant Vickery and I then made a 360 and launched another attack on the main formation. I damaged one with a few hits and drove up the rear of another, getting hits all over the ship. I believe the pilot and crew were killed, as the Ju 88 began smoking badly and went down out of control, with parts of the ship falling off. I broke off the attack and pulled out to the side before the third attack on the formation. I came in astern again. In this attack I plastered one 88, causing both engines to burn. The 88 disintegrated. I damaged a second, getting a few hits. I was out of ammunition, or so I thought, though later I learned that my guns on one side had a stoppage, and I had been hit in the engine from the rear gun position in one of the Ju 88s. My ship was covered with oil sprayed from the enemy aircraft that had been shot down, so I set course for home with Lieutenant Vickery, Lieutenant Greer having become separated. I claim three Ju 88s and one Me 109 destroyed and two Ju 88s damaged.

Ammunition: 1,540 rounds expended (API)

—Maj. George E. Preddy

```
TYPE OF MISSION: Combat
DATE: 6 August 1944
UNIT: 487th Fighter Squadron
TIME: 1110 to 1145 hours
LOCATION OF ACTION: Luneburg to Havelburg, 27,000
to 5,000 feet
WEATHER: 4/10 high cloud southeast of Hamburg,
visibility excellent
TYPE OF ENEMY AIRCRAFT ENCOUNTERED: Me 109
CLAIM: Six Me 109s destroyed
```

I was group leader. We were escorting the head combat wings of B-17s when 30-plus Me 109s in formation came into the third box from the south. We were at 1,000 feet above them, so I led White flight, consisting of Lieutenants Heyer and Doleac and myself, in astern of them. I opened fire on one of the rear 109s from 300 yards dead astern and got many hits around the cockpit.

Maj. George Preddy, getting in the cockpit for another combat mission, would become the highest-scoring Mustang pilot of World War II. *USAAF*

The 109 went down inverted, in flames. At this time Lieutenant Doleac became lost while shooting down an Me 109 that had gotten on Lieutenant Heyer's tail. Lieutenant Heyer and I continued our attack and I drove up behind another enemy aircraft, getting hits around the wing roots and setting him on fire after a short burst. He went spinning down, and the pilot bailed out after a few turns at 20,000 feet.

I saw Lieutenant Heyer, on my right, shoot down another 109. The enemy formation stayed together, taking practically no evasive action, and tried to get back for an attack on the bombers, which were off to the right. We continued with our attack on the rear end, and I fired on another from close range astern. He went down smoking badly, and I saw him begin to fall apart below us. At this time four other P-51s came in to help us with the attack. I fired at another 109, causing him to burn after a short burst. He spiraled down to the right in flames. The formation headed down in a left turn, still keeping themselves together in rather close formation. I got a good burst into another one, causing him to burn and spin down.

The enemy aircraft were down to 5,000 feet now, and one pulled off to the left. I was all alone with them now so went after this single 109 before he could get on my tail. I got an ineffective burst into him, causing him to smoke a little. I pulled up into a steep climb to the left above him and he climbed after me. I pulled in as tight as possible, climbing at 150 miles per hour. The Hun opened fire on me, but could not get enough deflection to do any damage. With my initial speed, I slightly outclimbed him. He fell off to the left and I dropped down astern of him. He jettisoned his canopy and I fired a short burst, getting many hits. As I pulled past, the pilot bailed out, at about 7,000 feet. I had lost all friendly and enemy aircraft so headed home alone. I claim six Me 109s destroyed.

Ammunition: 838 rounds (API) expended

—Maj. George E. Preddy

✪Col. David C. Schilling
22.5 Victories

Lt. Col. David Schilling of the 56th Fighter Group. Another top scorer with 22.5 victories, he would become C.O. of the group in August 1944. *USAAF*

David Carl Schilling was born on December 15, 1918, in Leavenworth, Kansas.

Schilling graduated from Dartmouth College in 1939 and soon after entered the Army Air Corps as a flying cadet. He graduated from pilot training on May 11, 1940, at Brooks Field, Texas. He joined the 56th Fighter Group and was initially in the 63rd Fighter Squadron. By March 1942 he was a captain, and joined the 62nd Fighter Squadron. Schilling was with the 56th in March 1943, when it became the first P-47 unit to enter combat. Schilling became the deputy group commander in August 1943 and took over leadership of the group in August 1944. He flew 132 combat missions before the end of the war.

Schilling remained in the Air Force following World War II and became CO of the 56th Fighter Group once more in 1946. Flying a Lockheed P-80, he took the unit on a trans-Atlantic flight to Germany in 1948. In 1950 he took a modified F-84 on a flight from London to Maine, refueling in the air, to chalk up the first fighter nonstop trans-Atlantic flight. He later took over command of the 31st Fighter Wing and took it on a number of historic flights.

Unfortunately, Schilling was killed in an automobile accident in England on August 14, 1956.

Decorations: Distinguished Service Cross with Oak Leaf Cluster, Silver Star with 2 Oak Leaf Clusters, Distinguished Flying Cross with 10 Oak Leaf Clusters, and Air Medal with 19 Oak Leaf Clusters.

Assigned aircraft in World War II:

P-47D 42-7938 HV-S, *Hewlett Woodmere, Long Island*

P-47D 42-75237 HV-S

P-47D 42-7523 HV-S, *Whack (Hairless Joe)*

P-47D 42-75541 HV-S, *Whack (Hairless Joe)*

P-47M 44-21125 HV-S

P-47D 42-26641 HV-S, *(Hairless Joe)*

```
TYPE OF MISSION:Combat
DATE:21 September 1944
UNIT:63rd Fighter Squadron, 56th Fighter Group
TIME:Approximately 1530 hours
LOCATION OF ACTION:Vicinity of Lochem, Holland
WEATHER:Overcast 3,000 to 4,000 feet;
visibility about 5 miles
TYPE OF ENEMY AIRCRAFT ENCOUNTERED:FW 190,
Me 109
CLAIM:Three FW 190s destroyed in the air
```

I was leading Daily White flight while patrolling an area about 20 miles east of Arnhem. As I crossed the small town of Lochem heading south, I saw one FW 190 and one Me 109 directly in front of me heading west. I immediately attacked the FW 190 and was approximately 700 yards from him when he broke up to the left. I opened fire and closed to about 500 yards when I saw a very heavy concentration of strikes all over the aircraft. At this time the aircraft had climbed to about 900 feet, where it did a half-roll and crashed into the ground and exploded.

Then, about two miles to the north, I saw a P-47 with an FW 190 on its tail about firing at it. I climbed to about 1,000 feet and as I approached, the FW 190 tried to climb away turning slightly left. I fired about a five-second burst, opening at about 700 yards, and got hits all over the aircraft. The pilot immediately bailed out, and the ship rolled over and burned.

I then saw an FW 190 heading east. As I turned right to get on his tail he broke right. I closed around the circle to about 400 yards and gave him a four-second burst at 45 degrees. I noticed a fair concentration of hits all over the aircraft, and he reversed his turn, spun, and crashed. I claim three FW 190s destroyed.

–Lt. Col. David C. Schilling

```
TYPE OF MISSION:Combat
DATE:26 November 1943
UNIT:61st Fighter Squadron, 56th Fighter Group
TIME:1206-1218 hours
LOCATION OF ACTION:Southeast of Oldenburg
WEATHER:5/10 stratocumulus, 12,000 feet down
TYPE OF ENEMY AIRCRAFT ENCOUNTERED-:FW
190, Me 210
CLAIM:Two FW 190s destroyed, one Me 210
damaged or probable, pending assessment
```

I was leading the group and flying Keyworth White One. When this group was still approximately 10 miles west of the bomber formation, an FW 190 flew under my flight, heading northwest. I did a slight turn left and got on his tail, approximately 1,000 yards behind him. He then did an aileron roll to the left, which was followed by a flick roll to the left, and he split-essed to the deck. By this time I had closed to approximately 800 yards and started down with him. Since we had not rendezvoused with the bombers, I immediately broke off to the right and proceeded toward the bombers. This airplane was carrying a belly tank and never jettisoned it.

Unobserved by me but seen by my wingman, second element leader, and Blue flight leader, a red chute appeared just as I broke off to proceed toward the bombers.

Several minutes later, several enemy aircraft were observed underneath our formation and heading toward the rear of the bombers. We bounced them and they dove down to 8,000 or 10,000 feet, and would zoom back up to reengage the squadron.

One of Lt. Col. David Schilling's aircraft. This one is *Wack*. Schilling flew two tours with the 56th Group. *USAAF*

Eventually I lost my wingman, and my second element had aborted. I sighted an FW 190 heading northwest across the rear of the bomber formation in a shallow dive. I immediately made a slight turn to the right and followed, closing fairly slowly. At an altitude of approximately 18,000 feet, I opened fire and eventually got the right deflection, which caused a heavy concentration of strikes on the top of the canopy, fuselage, and wing roots. Immediately a large flash issued, apparently from the wing roots and he slowly began to fall off to the right, pouring out a large trail of smoke. I last saw this plane going down perpendicularly, smoking.

I broke off the attack with a left chandelle and observed an Me 210 climbing very steeply just off my right wing several thousand feet below. I was then about 24,000 feet and going about 200 miles per hour. Upon sighting this aircraft I winged over to the right and closed to about 600 to 700 yards and opened fire. A fair concentration of hits were observed at the rear of the canopy and fuselage, and he flicked over and started straight down. At this time, I pushed the nose down and attempted a deflection shot, but observed no hits. About that time, an enemy aircraft had cruised up my rear and opened fire. I immediately zoomed up to the left and lost this aircraft. I never saw this aircraft, and its position was only made known by its tracers. I therefore claim two FW 190s destroyed and one Me 210 damaged or probable, pending assessments.

Ammunition: 1,048 rounds expended (.50-caliber API)

–Lt. Col. David C. Schilling

```
TYPE OF MISSION: Combat
DAT: 23 December 1944
UNIT: 62nd Fighter Squadron
TIME: Approx. 1145 hours
LOCATION OF ACTION: Vicinity of Bonn/Koblenz area
(Euskirchen A/D)
WEATHER: Hazy, scattered clouds
TYPE OF ENEMY AIRCRAFT ENCOUNTERED: Me 109,
FW 190
CLAIM: Three Me 109s, Two FW 190s destroyed
```

As the Group reached a location approximately 30 miles west of Bonn at an altitude of 27,000 feet. Control changed our previous vector of 103 degrees to 90 degrees magnetic, telling us that a large number of enemy aircraft were ahead to the east. In about two minutes, a gaggle was sighted about 10 miles to the north, flying west. We turned to a vector of 330 degrees in an effort to cut them off, but they managed to get away in a large patch of cirrus clouds. We then returned to the vector of 90 degrees and in one or two minutes sighted another large gaggle about 10 miles to the south with a heading of west. We turned south but lost them the same as the first.

I then called MEW and asked them why they had not picked the enemy aircraft up and to give us some help. Their reply was, "Don't worry, there are plenty straight east at 22,000 to 23,000 feet." Two or three minutes later, the 63rd Squadron leader called and said a large formation of FWs was directly below us. At the same time I sighted approximately 40 enemy aircraft flying south in a wide turn to the left, about 1,500 feet below us and several miles ahead. I told the 63rd to attack and the 61st to aid, as I was going to hit the enemy aircraft ahead, since we had altitude and speed on both enemy formations.

I flew straight ahead, pulled up, applied full power, and made a slow diving turn to the left to position my flight on the outside and to bring as many planes into position to fire as possible. In so doing, I managed to hit the right rear Me 109 with about a 20-degree deflection shot at a range of about 700 yards. There was a large concentration of strikes all over the fuselage, and he fell off to the left. I then picked out another more or less ahead of the first and fired from about the same range. He caught fire immediately.

By this time, the first Me 109 was slightly ahead, below and to the left, at which point he started to smoke and catch on fire. I then picked another and fired at about 1,000 yards. I missed as he broke right and started to dive for the deck. At about 17,000 feet, I closed to about 500 yards and fired, resulting in a heavy concentration of strikes and the pilot bailing out.

Hairless Joe with the mighty club was a cartoon character that graced the aircraft flown by Lt. Col. Schilling. Schilling got his five in one day on December 23, 1944, flying this aircraft. USAAF

At this point I had become separated from the other three flights and had only my own with me. I heard Major Comstock of the 63rd Squadron in a hell of a fight, and called to get his position. As I was attempting to locate him, I sighted another gaggle of 35 to 40 FW 190s 1,000 feet below and circling to the left. I requested the same tactics as before and attacked one from 500 yards and slightly above and to the left. This plane immediately began to smoke and burn, spinning off to the left. I then fired at a second FW and only got two or three strikes. He immediately took violent evasive actions and it took me several minutes of maneuvering until I managed to get in a position to fire. I fired from about 300 yards from above and to the left, forcing me to pull through him and fire as he went out of sight over the cowling. I gave about a five-second burst and began getting strikes all over him. The pilot immediately bailed out and the ship spun down to the left, smoking and burning until it blew up at about 15,000 feet.

By this time I was alone and saw a lone 63rd plane. I called and he joined up just as a 35- to 40-plane formation of FWs flew by, heading west about 1,000 feet above. I had hoped to sneak by them and turn upon their tails but they saw me just as I started my climbing turn. I knew I would have to hit the deck sooner or later, but thought I could get their tail-end man before I had to. My wingman lagged back and just as I was getting set, he called and said two were on his tail. I thought I saw him get hit and told him to do vertical aileron rolls to the deck. At that time two got behind me and were getting set, so I did several rolls as I started down. I hit the switch and outran them by a mile as I got to the deck. I lost them and zoomed back to 8,000 feet.

I then called Major Comstock and told him to assume command and his reply was that he was in my predicament, so I called Captain Perry and repeated the order with the same answer. I then called the boys and told them to break it off and return to base.

–Lt. Col. David C. Schilling

✪Capt. John F. Thornell Jr.
17.25 Victories

The fact that Lt. John Thornell was only a lieutenant in a group with Lt. Col. J. C. Meyer and Maj. George Preddy seemed to have knocked him out of the limelight. *USAAF*

John Francis Thornell Jr. was born in Stoughton, Massachusetts, on April 19, 1921.

Thornell entered the U.S. Army Air Force in 1942 and graduated from flight school on February 16, 1943, at Craig Field, Alabama. He joined the 328th Fighter Squadron of the 352nd Fighter Group at the end of December 1943. During his combat tour he accounted for 17.25 kills from January 30, 1944, through June 21, 1944.

Thornell stayed on the Air Force following World War II and retired as a lieutenant colonel in July 1971.

Decorations: Distinguished Service Cross, Silver Star, Distinguished Flying Cross with 5 Oak Leaf Clusters, and Air Medal with 4 Oak Leaf Clusters.

Assigned aircraft in World War II:

P-47D 42-22474 PE-I, *Pattie*

P-51B 42-106872 PR-T, *Pattie II*

```
TYPE OF MISSION: Combat
DATE: 19 April 1944
UNIT: 328th Fighter Squadron
TIME: 1030 hours
LOCATION OF ACTION: 10-15 miles southwest of Kassel
WEATHER: CAVU-Light scattered clouds
TYPE OF ENEMY AIRCRAFT ENCOUNTERED-FW 190
CLAIM: Two FW 190s destroyed
```

I was flying Yellow Three position. When we made rendezvous with the bombers and noticed high contrails, we went to climb. After the bombers hit the target, we saw about seven FW 190s high. I couldn't climb fast enough, so I became lost from my flight. At about 1030 hours, I found myself alone with seven FW 190s queued up on a straggling B-17, which had just fallen out of formation at about 22,000 feet and was losing altitude.

I bounced the FW 190s, becoming eighth man in the queue. I hit the last man and the others broke into me. The bomber was hit badly and the crew bailed out. A red-nosed P-51 joined me, and we continued our combat with the seven FW 190s from 24,000 feet to the deck. I fired at 20,000 feet, hitting an FW 190. The pilot jettisoned his canopy and started to bail out. I was about 50 to 60 yards out to one side and saw him fall back in the cockpit. His 190 spun through the overcast at 3,000 feet.

While in the dogfight at altitude, one FW 190 went by me so I fired a short burst and observed strikes on its fuselage and tail. After observing it spin through the overcast, I found myself with three FW 190s behind me, so I started to turn, but my aircraft went into a spin. I recovered at about 10,000 feet; the FW 190s were still with me. I turned into one and got on his tail and chased him to the deck, only giving him short bursts. On the deck, the pilot must have realized I was behind him. While he was looking around, his plane crashed into a tree, cartwheeled across a field, and exploded. I went back and took a picture of the wreckage, and then came home alone.

Ranges were from 500 up to 200 yards and deflection was 30 degrees to zero for all my firing. When I was fairly close to one of the FW 190s, I noticed something under the fuselage, which made the 190 resemble a P-51 from a side view. I later noticed it on two or three of the other FW 190s. I claim two FW 190s destroyed and one FW 190 damaged.

Ammunition: 358 rounds expended

—1st Lt. John F. Thornell Jr.

```
✿ TYPE OF MISSION: Combat              ✿
  DATE: 8 May 1944
  UNIT: 328th Fighter Squadron, 352nd Fighter Group
  TIME: Approx. 1000 hours
  LOCATION OF ACTION: Area of Nienburg
  WEATHER: 5-7/10 from 1,500 to 5,000 feet
  TYPE OF ENEMY AIRCRAFT ENCOUNTERED: Me 109
  CLAIM: Three Me 109s destroyed
✿                                      ✿
```

I was leading Blue Section and made a bounce on four Me 109s that had just attacked the bombers from above. This was 20 minutes after rendezvous, and we had a dogfight. I fired a one-second burst at almost a head-on pass, observing no hits but breaking up their formation as they hit the deck. My wingman, Lieutenant Galiga, shot one Me 109 off my tail.

After this combat I was alone at 5,000 feet, my flight having been separated in the fight. I joined up with White Leader

(Lieutenant Colonel Meyer). We spotted three Me 109s drawing contrails and heading for the bombers. They broke for the deck and we followed. I was in the lead on the bounce.

At 50 to 100 yards range, I opened fire on the number -two man in the enemy formation. He burst into flames and hit the ground. I was down at 200 feet by then. I then slid over and fired at the number -one Me 109. He fell apart in the air, and the fuselage hit the ground and exploded.

We started for home but I lost White Leader in the clouds. When I was at 3,000 feet I observed an Me 109 on my tail. Thinking I was out of ammo, I called to Colonel Meyer but he couldn't find me. I was turning with this Me 109 at this time. Colonel Meyer called and said to chew his tail off because I was close enough. As I turned inside the 109, I closed to 15 yards, when he immediately bailed out.

I dropped below the clouds, saw his chute open, and saw him land in the woods. To the left I observed a field that I believe to be Bomlitz, with five Me 109s parked on it. I observed another chute coming down on the field. I flew over and saw the man was an American. He landed on the edge of the enemy airfield. At this time the flak and light gun fire was pretty heavy, so I turned and headed for home, climbing to 10,000 feet to cross out. I claim three Me 109s destroyed.

Ammunition: 650 rounds expended

—1st Lt. John F. Thornell Jr.

✪Capt. Ray S. Wetmore
21.25 Victories

This photo of Capt. Raymond S. Wetmore and his crew chief was probably taken shortly after January 14, 1945, when he got the five in one day, just after his return for a second tour with the 359th Fighter Group. Wetmore would have 21.25 kills by the end of the war. *359th Fighter Group Association*

Ray Shuey Wetmore was born on September 30, 1923, in Kerman, California.

Wetmore entered the U.S. Army Air Corps in 1941 and became an aviation cadet in July 1942. He graduated from flight school on March 30, 1943, at Moore Field, Texas. In April 1943 he was assigned to the 370th Fighter Squadron of the 359th Fighter Group. He flew two tours of combat with this unit and at the close of his second tour he was a captain with 21.25 victories. He was promoted to major in July 1945.

Wetmore remained in the Air Force and was CO of the 59th Fighter Squadron, 33rd Fighter Group, when he was killed flying an F-86 on February 14, 1951.

Decorations: Distinguished Service Cross with Oak Leaf Cluster, Silver Star with Oak Leaf Cluster, Distinguished Flying Cross with 5 Oak Leaf Clusters, and Air Medal with 11 Oak Leaf Clusters.

Aircraft assigned in World War II:

P-47D 42-75068 CS-P

P-51B 42-106894 CS-P

P-51D 44-14733, *Daddy's Girl*

```
TYPE OF MISSION: Combat
DATE: 2 November 1944
UNIT: 370th Fighter Squadron
TIME: 1245 hours
LOCATION OF ACTION: Vicinity of Erfurt-Weimar-Jena
WEATHER: 7/10 cloud
TYPE OF ENEMY AIRCRAFT ENCOUNTERED: Me 109
CLAIM: Two Me 109s destroyed in the air
```

I was leading Red Section, escorting bombers over Merseburg, when approximately 30 Me 109s attacked the bombers. We were on the box of bombers ahead. I called my section and told them to drop their tanks, then half-rolled to intercept the bandits as they split-essed through their formation, but our speed was so great we didn't have a chance to fire. This split the Jerrys up, so I singled out one Me 109 and closed to about 400 yards before opening fire. I was using the new K-14 sight, and as soon as I pulled the trigger I saw many strikes around the wing roots and fuselage. The German pilot dropped his flaps to slow down so he could split-ess. My speed was still around 450, and I soon overran him. I got in another burst before doing this. He went down in a barrel roll straight through the overcast with me following at a very close range. His roll developed into a spin and he never pulled out. By this time, my wingman had engaged another Me 109 who was on his tail, so I was alone below the overcast. Before I had a chance to climb back up through the overcast at 6,000 feet, 15 to 20 Me 109s bounced me. I immediately went into a tight turn and started calling for help. The German pilots seemed very aggressive but very innocent about fighter tactics, for they never did take advantage of the position. During the Lufbery, I fired at the Jerry at about 70 degrees deflection. I noticed three strikes on the cockpit. By this time the other Jerrys seem to have disappeared, so I continued my attack on this one. I never did get another shot on him for evidently I hit the pilot on the first burst. The plane went into a stall and tumbled right into the ground. The location was near a small town with a lot of small arms fire, and it was getting pretty hot around there. During the fight I saw a B-17 come down through the overcast with wing fires. The Jerrys continued to make attacks on it, and I couldn't help them because I had a fight of my own.

Ammunition: 294 rounds (API) expended

—Capt. Ray S. Wetmore

```
TYPE OF MISSION:Combat
DATE:27 November 1944
UNIT:370th Fighter Squadron
TIME:1245 to 1300 hours
LOCATION OF ACTION:Vicinity southeast of Hanover
WEATHER:Fair
TYPE OF ENEMY AIRCRAFT ENCOUNTERED:Me 109
CLAIM:Three Me 109s destroyed in the air
```

I was leading Red flight when Nuthouse vectored the operation to north of Munster, where bandits were reported. The squadron got split up due to some intense flak. I took my flight to the vicinity of our strafing target, hoping to rendezvous with the squadron again. At this time I saw two gaggles of approximately 100 planes each. One bunch was Me 109s and the other FW 190s. I immediately started calling our group and notifying Nuthouse as to the position, altitude, and direction they were flying. I continued to follow them, remaining high and to the rear of their formation. A few minutes later my second element had to return home due to engine trouble. By this time the Jerrys found out I was there and started out sending four ship flights after us. I continued to call in the Jerrys' position until we had to bounce them to save our own necks,

Capt. Wetmore runs up his personal aircraft, *Daddy's Girl*, late in the war. The scoreboard seems to indicate that just about his full score has been painted on. *USAAF*

as they were beginning to bounce us. I closed in on an Me 109 to approximately 600 yards before firing. I was using a K-14 sight. As soon as I started firing, this Me 109 burst into flames and went down spinning. I claim this enemy aircraft as destroyed. At the same time, I saw my wingman, Lieutenant York, hit another Me 109 and it went down spinning, pouring out black smoke. I then broke into the Jerrys bouncing us. I got a good burst at one from 300 yards with a 20-degree deflection. The enemy aircraft lit up with strikes and went into a tumble, pouring out black smoke. The last time I saw the Me 109 it was in flames, spinning. I claim this enemy aircraft as destroyed. I saw another Jerry making a pass on me so I turned into him. We went around and around from 30,000 feet to the deck. He seemed very aggressive and was darn good with his Me 109. Although I could outturn him he was on my tail a lot of times. He seemed to make good use of his fowler flaps. I finally ran out of ammo but by this time I had hit him several times. I made another pass at him and he bailed out. I then took a picture of him in his chute. Then, for the next 10 minutes, I was attacked repeatedly by FW 190s, but managed to outmaneuver them. They finally broke off, and I came home. I claim three Me 109s destroyed in the air.

Ammunition: 1,243 rounds (API) expended

–Capt. Ray S. Wetmore

```
TYPE OF MISSION: Combat
DATE: 14 January 1945
UNIT: 370th Fighter Squadron
TIME: 1330-1400 hours
LOCATION OF ACTION: Vicinity of Vorden airfield West
of Dummer Lake
WEATHER: CAVU
TYPE OF ENEMY AIRCRAFT ENCOUNTERED: FW 190
CLAIM: Four FW 190s destroyed in the air, one FW 190
destroyed in the air shared
```

I was leading Red Section going to rendezvous east of Hanover, when I when I noticed a bogie in front of me doing lazy eights and chandelles. I turned into the plane, and he started climbing, going on a 20-degree heading. I called my flight and told them to drop their tanks, and I started after him at full power. He ran away from us as if we were standing still. I followed him all the way to Dummer Lake, then gave up the chase. At this time Nuthouse called and said bandits were taking off from an airfield 22 miles northwest of Dummer Lake. I took my flight up that way but couldn't find anything. I then turned back toward Dummer Lake and at this time Nuthouse said bandits were in the near vicinity. I saw a Lufbery low at two o'clock. Just then four FW 190s went below me in trail and we made the bounce. I caught the Jerrys on the deck and picked my target. I closed to about 300 yards with 20-degrees deflection and fired a long burst with excellent results. One landing gear came down and the Hun tried to belly in and succeeded in creaming himself and the airplane too. I claim this FW 190 destroyed.

I chose another 190 and gave him a short burst from dead astern at very short range. He tried to break but snapped into the ground, exploding. I claim this enemy aircraft destroyed. There were still two FW 190s in the formation and I called my wingman to take the one of the port side and I would take the other one. I made a pass at my Jerry from dead astern. I fired from about 300 yards, getting many strikes. He went into a spin and spun straight into the ground. I claim this FW 190 destroyed. Just then I saw my wingman making a pass on his target but his windshield was all frosted up and he couldn't see his gunsight. I got the Jerry off and we had him in a crossfire, both of us getting a lot of strikes. The German bellied his aircraft in an open snow-covered field. At this time I told my wingman to strafe the German. He called back and said he couldn't see out of his canopy. So I fired, killing the pilot and setting the airplane on fire. I claim this FW 190 destroyed, shared with Lieutenant Russchenberg. We then joined up and climbed to altitude. Just then I saw two more FW 190s. As I started to make my pass, a P-51 with a red-checkered nose made a pass on the first Jerry, with good results. The German had to bail out. I fired at the second German from about 400 yards with 30-degrees deflection. I got several strikes and the Jerry jettisoned his canopy and bailed out. I claim this FW 190 destroyed. I claim four FW 190s destroyed in the air and one FW 190 destroyed in the air, shared with Lieutenant Russchenberg.

Ammunition: 1,324 rounds (API) expended

–*Capt. Ray S. Wetmore*

✪Capt. William T. Whisner

15.5 Victories

Lt. William T. Whisner of the 487th Fighter Squadron. Lt. Whisner flew wingman to Maj. George Preddy for a while and then came into his own. He is shown here with *Princess Elizabeth*, with which he was not greatly pleased. *USAAF*

William Thomas Whisner was born on October 17, 1923, in Shreveport, Louisiana.

Whisner left Centenary College to enter the U.S. Army Air Corps in March 1942. He graduated from flight school on February 16, 1943, at Napier Field, Alabama, and shortly thereafter joined the 487th Fighter Squadron of the 352nd Fighter Group. Whisner flew two combat tours with the unit. He really came into his own after flying for some months as wingman for Maj. George Preddy. He finished the war as a captain with 15.5 aerial victories.

Whisner left the Air Force at the end of the war but returned in October 1947. In September 1951, during the Korean Conflict, he joined the 334th Fighter Squadron of the Fourth Fighter Interceptor Wing. During his time with this unit, he was credited with downing two MiG 15s. In November 1951, Whisner transferred to the 51st Fighter Interceptor Wing, where he became the unit's first ace on February 23, 1952.

Whisner continued his career in the Air Force in various fighter units and staff assignments, during which he attained the rank of colonel. He retired from the Air Force in 1971.

Whisner died of an allergic reaction to an insect sting on July 21, 1989.

Decorations: (World War II): Distinguished Service Cross with Oak Leaf Cluster, Silver Star, Distinguished Flying Cross with 3 Oak Leaf Clusters, and Air Medal with 12 Oak Leaf Clusters; (Korea): Distinguished Service Cross, Bronze Star Medal, and Distinguished Flying Cross.

Assigned aircraft in World War II:

P-47D 42-8404, *Beverly*

P-51 42-106449 HO-W, *Princess Elizabeth*

P-51D 44-14237 HO-W, *Moonbeam McSwine*

```
TYPE OF MISSION: Combat
DATE: 21 November 1944
UNIT: 487th Fighter Squadron
TIME: 1230 to 1250 hours
LOCATION OF ACTION: Southwest Mersburg, at 25,000 feet
WEATHER: Heavy haze layer from 18,000 to 20,000
feet
TYPE OF ENEMY AIRCRAFT ENCOUNTERE: FW 190
CLAIM: Six FW 190s destroyed, one FW 190 probably
destroyed
```

I was leading Green flight in a six-ship section, with Colonel Meyer leading Black flight, the section. Black Three and Four aborted, and my flight became Black Three, Four, Five, and Six.

At approximately 1225 we saw a gaggle of 50-plus enemy aircraft flying on an interception course to the last box of bombers, which had already left the target. We were climbing at 23,000 and immediately started after them wide open, closing in behind them at 29,000 feet. Major Preddy, leading a five-ship section from the 328th Squadron, was close behind us.

Twenty-plus enemy aircraft were flying in close formation, with six-ship cover flights. The cover flights were flying fairly wide, above, to the sides, and to the rear of the main formation. As we approached from the rear, these cover flights began essing. I identified them as FW 190s and saw that they all had belly tanks.

Colonel Meyer told me to take a straggler who was on the starboard and rear of the formation. As I closed on him the formation turned about 35 degrees right, and this straggler joined the formation. I fired a short burst at this 190 at about 400 yards, using the K-14, but observed no strikes. I closed to 200 yards and fired another burst, which covered him with strikes. Large pieces flew off and he fell into a spin, smoking and burning. I closed on another 190 and hit him with a good burst from about 150 yards, knocking pieces off. He fell off to the right, and I hit him again at 15 or 20 degrees deflection from 100 yards or less. Again pieces came off, and he fell into a flat spin. I watched this one go through a haze layer, still spinning and smoking. About this time the enemy seemed to be tired. I saw them break off and dive down, taking violent evasive action. I did not attempt to follow them but stayed behind the formation. I closed up behind a three-ship flight, which was flying almost line-abreast about 50 yards apart. I put my sight on the leader, but before I opened fire he broke down. I was then almost between the other two. I banked steeply to the right, then back to the left, and hit the one on the right at less than 100 yards. Pieces flew off him and he fell off into a flat spin, smoking and burning. I was depending on my

Capt. William Whisner was much more at home and scored most of his victories in *Moonbeam McSwine,* named for a lovely Dogpatch damsel from the comic strips. *USAAF*

wingman, Lieutenant Waldron, to get the one on the left, and he didn't fail me. I saw him hit the 190, which went down out of control, smoking.

I closed on another 190, which was turning from left to right. He saw me and turned steeply to the right. I cut him off and hit him all over in a deflection shot of 15 to 20 degrees or less. He went down in a vertical dive, puffing smoke and flame, and disappeared into the haze. At this time, I saw another 190 going down in flames. My wingman had gotten this one. I made a 180-degree turn right while watching him and lost my wingman. The main formation of 190s was still intact, but only two ships remained in the cover section. I firewalled everything and caught up with them fast. I picked the last one, fired at him from

300 yards. Due to heavy contrails, I did not see any strikes on him. He snapped into a flat spin and went below me. I claim a probable on this one. I was very close to the main formation at this time. I picked out one of them and started firing from about 200 yards. He was completely covered with strikes and fell off into a dive. I turned and watched him and he broke into several pieces. I think the belly tank exploded. Up to this time, most of the 190s had dropped their belly tanks. I had plenty of time to plan my attacks, and those tanks made the 190s extremely vulnerable. As I fired on this last one, the main formation dropped their tanks and dived down and to the left.

I followed but lost them in the haze. As I pulled up, I saw three of the 190s behind me so I stood my plane on its tail. At about 23,000 feet, I saw a 190 on a P-51's tail. I attacked him and fired a deflection shot from 100 yards. As I mushed past his line of flight, he flew through my fire. He then leveled off and I hit him from slightly above at 50 yards. My fire hit him in the engine and cockpit. His canopy came off, along with other large pieces. He went straight down with his engine smoking and burning. I joined Colonel Meyer and my wingman and came out with them.

My individual events in this report are true and correct, but I am not positive about the sequence of events (with the exception of the last 190 I attacked and the probable). I claim six FW 190s destroyed and one FW 190 probably destroyed.

Ammunition: 1,385 rounds (API) expended

–*Capt. William T. Whisner*

```
TYPE OF MISSION:Combat
DATE:1 January 1945
UNIT:487th Fighter Squadron, 352nd Fighter Group
TIME:0930 hours
LOCATION OF ACTION:North of Leige, 2,000 feet to
deck
TYPE OF ENEMY AIRCRAFT ENCOUNTERED:Me 109,
FW 190
CLAIM:Two Me 109s, two FW 190s destroyed
```

I was leading Red flight. As we were taxiing out to the strip, I saw some air activity east of the field. The squadron, consisting of three four-ship flights, was taking off singly. As I started down the strip, Colonel Meyer called the controller and inquired about bandits in the vicinity. As I pulled my wheels up, the controller reported that there were bandits east of the field. We didn't take time to form up, but set course, wide open, straight for the bandits. There were a few P-47s mixing it up with the bandits as I arrived. I ran into about 30 190s at 1,500 feet. There were many 109s above them. I picked out a 190 and pressed the trigger. Nothing happened. I reached down and turned on my gun switch and gave him a couple of good bursts. As I watched him hit the ground and explode, I felt myself being hit. I broke sharply to the right, and up. A 190 was about 50 yards behind me, firing away. As I was turning with him another P-51 attacked him and he broke off this attack on me. I then saw that I had several 20-millimeter holes in each wing and another hit in my oil tank. My left aileron control was also out. I was losing oil but my temperature and pressure were steady. Being over friendly territory I could see no reason for landing immediately, so turned toward a big dogfight and shortly had another 190 in my sights. After I hit him several times, he attempted to bail out. I gave him a burst as he raised up, and he went down with his plane, which exploded and burned. There were several 109s in the vicinity, so I engaged one of them. We fought for 5 or 10 minutes, and I finally managed to get behind him. I hit him good and the pilot bailed out at 200 feet. I clobbered him as he bailed out, and he tumbled into the ground. At this time I saw 15 or 20 fires from crashed planes. Bandits were reported strafing the field, so I headed for the strip. I saw a 109 strafe the northeast end of the strip. I started after him and he turned into me. We made two head-on passes, and on the second pass, I hit him in the nose and wings. He crashed and burned east of the strip. I chased several more bandits but they evaded in the clouds. I had oil on my windshield and canopy so came back to the strip and landed.

All of the enemy pilots were very aggressive and extremely good. I am very happy that we were able to shoot down 23 with a loss of none. We were outnumbered five to one, with full fuselage tanks. The P-47s on this field did a fine job and helped us considerably. The cooperation among our fighters was extremely good, and we did the job as a team. I claim two Me 109s destroyed and two FW 190s destroyed.

–*Capt. William T. Whisner*

✪Captain Charles E. Yeager
11.5 Victories

Lt. Charles "Chuck" Yeager had to go all the way to the top to get permission to fly combat again after evading capture, but General Eisenhower finally approved it. He went on to score 11.5 victories before the war's end. *USAAF*

Charles "Chuck" Elwood Yeager was born on February 13, 1923, in Myra, West Virginia.

Yeager joined the U.S. Air Corps in September 1941. He later entered flight training and graduated on March 10, 1943, at Luke Field, Arizona. He was assigned to the 363rd Fighter Squadron of the 357th Fighter Group. Yeager was shot down flying a P-51 Mustang on March 5, 1944. He managed to evade capture and returned to England in May 1944. In July 1944,

General Eisenhower granted permission for Yeager to return to combat duty. Yeager downed 11.5 enemy aircraft and attained the rank of captain.

Following the war, Yeager became a test pilot at Muroc Air Force Base, California. On October 14, 1947, flying the Bell XS-1, Yeager became the first man to break the sound barrier. Later assigned to a number of tactical fighter units, Yeager flew combat once more, this time over Vietnam. He retired from the Air Force a brigadier general on March 1, 1975.

Decorations: (World War II): Silver Star with Oak Leaf Cluster, Distinguished Flying Cross, Bronze Star Medal, Air Medal with 6 Oak Leaf Clusters, and Purple Heart; (Postwar): Distinguished Service Medal, Legion of Merit with Oak Leaf Cluster, Distinguished Flying Cross with Oak Leaf Cluster, and Air Medal with 3 Oak Leaf Clusters.

Assigned aircraft in World War II:

P-51B 43-6763 B6-Y, *Glamorous Glen*

P-51D 44-13897 B6-Y, *Glamorous Glen II*

P-51D 44-14888 B6-Y, *Glamorous Glen III*

```
TYPE OF MISSION: Combat
DATE: 12 October 1944
UNIT: 363rd Fighter Squadron, 357th Fighter Group
TIME: 1130 hours
LOCATION OF ACTION: Steinhudder Lake
WEATHER: 5/10 cumulus from 3,000 to 5,000 feet
TYPE OF ENEMY AIRCRAFT ENCOUNTERED: Me 109
CLAIM: Five Me 109s destroyed
```

I was leading the group with Cement Squadron and was roving out to the right of the first box of bombers. I was over Steinhudder Lake when 22 Me 109s crossed in front of my squadron from 11 o'clock. I was coming out of the sun and they were about 1-1/2 miles away at the same level of 28,000 feet. I fell in

Glamorous Glen III was Capt. Charles Yeager's last Mustang. He may have scored his Me 262 kill and his five FW 190s in one day in this bird. *USAAF*

behind the enemy formation and followed them for about three minutes, climbing to 30,000 feet. I still had my wing tanks and had closed to l,000 yards, opening within firing range, and positioning the squadron behind the entire enemy formation. Two of the Me 109s were lagging over to the right. One slowed up, and before I could start firing, rolled over and the pilot bailed out. The pilot of the other Me 109, flying his wing, bailed out immediately after, as I was ready to line him in my sights. I was the closest to the tail end of the enemy formation, and no one else was in shooting range and no one was firing. I dropped my tanks and then closed up to the closest Jerry and opened fire from 600 yards, using the K-14 sight. I observed strikes all over the ship, particularly heavy in the cockpit. He skidded off to the left and was smoking and streaming coolant, and went into a slow diving turn to the left. I was closing up on another Me 109 so I did not follow him down. Lieutenant Stern, flying in Blue Flight, reported that the 109 was on fire as it passed him and went into a spin. I closed up on the next Me 109 to 100 yards, skidded to the right and took a deflection shot of about 10 degrees. I gave about a three-second burst and the whole fuselage split open and blew up after he passed.

Another Me 109 to the right had cut his throttle and was trying to get behind. I broke to the right and quickly pulled to the left on his tail. He started pulling it in and I was pulling 6 Gs. I got a lead from about 300 yards and gave him a short burst. There were hits on his wings and tail section. He snapped to the right three times and bailed out when he quit snapping at around 18,000 feet. I did not black out during the engagement due the efficiency of the "G" suit. Even though I was skidding, I hit the second Me 109 by keeping the bead and range on the enemy aircraft. In my estimation, the K-14 sight is the biggest improvement to combat equipment for fighters up to this date.

The Me 109s appeared to have a type of bubble canopy. They had purple noses and were a mousy brown all over. I claim five Me 109s destroyed.

Ammunition: 587 rounds expended (.50 caliber)

—Lt. Charles E. Yeager

✪Col. Hubert Zemke
17.75 Victories

Col. Hubert Zemke was a disciplinarian and a very aggressive pilot, just what was needed for a fighter group. He left the 56th Group to lead the 479th Fighter Group, but was caught in a violent storm and had to bail out, joining the POW ranks. *USAAF*

Col. Hubert Zemke was born in Missoula, Montana, on March 14, 1914. Zemke joined the U.S. Army Air Corps as a flying cadet in February 1936 and graduated from flight training on June 20, 1937. He served with the Eighth Pursuit Group at Langley Field, Virginia, for some time before being sent to England as an observer during the early part of World War II. From England he was assigned to Russia, where, as an assistant air attaché, he taught Russian pilots to fly the Curtis P-40.

Promotion came quickly to Zemke. He was a major when he was assigned to the new 56th Fighter Group in September 1942, and he was promoted to lieutenant colonel a month later. He trained his men on the new Republic P-47 Thunderbolt and took them overseas to the Eighth Air Force in England in January 1943. The unit flew its first combat mission on April 13, 1943. The 56th Fighter Group became an outstanding group in the Eighth Air

Force and was credited with the highest number of aerial victories of any of its fighter units. Its success was largely due to the leadership of Colonel Zemke.

Zemke left the 56th Group on August 12, 1944, and assumed command of the 479th Fighter Group. On October 30, 1944, he was caught in a violent storm over Germany and was forced to bail out. He was captured by the Germans and became the ranking officer among prisoners of war in Stalag Luft I at Barth, Germany. Following liberation in May 1945, he negotiated the return of his fellow prisoners to England, rather than being processed through Russia, as their liberators were demanding. Zemke remained in the service following World War II. He commanded several fighter units before he retired from the Air Force in July 1966. As a civilian, he became a gunsmith and later an almond grower in Oroville, California. Zemke died of pneumonia at his home on August 30, 1994.

Decorations: Distinguished Service Cross, Silver Star, Distinguished Flying Cross with 7 Oak Leaf Clusters, and Air Medal with 2 Oak Leaf Clusters.

Known assigned aircraft in World War II:

P-47C 41-6330 LM-Z, *Mon Tobapn III*

P-47D 42-75864 UN-Z

P-47D 42-26414 UN-Z

```
TYPE OF MISSION: Combat
DATE: 12 May 1944
UNIT: 63rd Fighter Squadron, 56th Fighter Group
TIME: 1145 hours
LOCATION OF ACTION: 310 miles south to south-
southwest of Koblenz, Germany
WEATHER: Clear with a bad haze layer from 12,000
feet down
TYPE OF ENEMY AIRCRAFT ENCOUNTERED: Me 109
CLAIM: One Me 109 destroyed
```

Because of the peculiar circumstances of this mission, the narrative in my mind began much earlier than just the last battle and destruction of the Me 109 claimed destroyed.

Three of us—Lt. Col. Preston Piper, 2nd Lt. W. D. Johnson, and myself—had moved out to scout an area north of Frankfurt, when we were bounced from above by seven Me 109s. During this engagement, my two wingmen were shot down. I have no idea of how many the two pilots may have damaged or even destroyed, but I believe there were some. My escape was by outspinning and outdiving the enemy. As I flew westward toward home, another four Me 109s jumped me over Weisbaden. In the ensuing defensive battle, I was again just able to elude the enemy. After outrunning these aircraft, a course of 290 degrees was again set for England.

South of Koblenz about four enemy aircraft were seen circling at 15,000 feet, my altitude at the time being approximately 20,000 feet. My first intention at the moment was to bounce these planes by having the superior altitude and pulling off home. I had hardly circled before several more FW 190s and Me 109s were seen to assemble with the original four. Gradually their strength built up until an estimated 30 enemy aircraft were circling below and gradually increasing their altitude as they assembled.

I continued to circle them, calling to the other members of the 56th Fighter Group, who were spread in the Koblenz-Frankfurt area, for help. My purpose was to pull a kill on these enemy aircraft.

For more than 15 minutes I continued to circle above this concentration. As they climbed, I moved up until my final altitude was approximately 29,000 feet. At this point I was finally throwing contrails, which were picked up by Lieutenant Rankin and his wingman, Lieutenant Clem C. Thornton. These two pilots moved up to within a half-mile, and I told them to give me top cover while I bounced the enemy circling below.

The dive was fairly steep, and a lonesome Me 109 was picked up on this outer portion of the Lufbery below. By this time I was in firing position. He presented a 60- to-90-degree deflection shot and over two rings of lead were laid off before squeezing the trigger. The fire of my tracers was well ahead of him and I allowed him to fly through the bullet pattern. At no time did I see a terrific explosion, but several hits were seen over the entire length of the fuselage.

At the point where I was about to ram him, I pulled the attack back abruptly, and my airplane zoomed up into a climbing turn. Looking back, I saw the Me 109 do two sloppy flick rolls, which wound up in a spin. The engine burst into flames, and the pilot bailed out. This fact was announced over the radio just soon enough for me to hear Lieutenant Rankin tell me to "break left," as an Me 109 was on my tail. This plane was never seen, for Lieutenant Rankin was down on top of my position and away,

Col. Zemke on the wing of *Mon Tobapn III*. Zemke had trained Russian P-40 pilots before he got the 56th Group. Note the "wheel" on the nose of the aircraft, further noting that this is the boss' airplane. *USAAF*

just as I entered combat with four more Me 109s. However, seen far below during this combat, I saw an airplane on fire that was spinning down. This may have been the enemy aircraft Lieutenant Rankin shot off my tail. My further action was to break into the four Me 109s, do a half-roll to the west and outrun them. The gasoline gauge registered but 125 gallons of gasoline, so after the last enemy fighters gave up, I cut everything back to the absolute minimum and moved off home by myself.

–*Col. Hubert Zemke*

```
TYPE OF MISSION:Combat
DATE:7 June 1944
UNIT:61st Fighter Squadron, 56th Fighter Group
TIME:Approximately 1840-1900 hours
LOCATION OF ACTION:In the triangle between
Chartres, Etempes-Mondesir, and Paris
WEATHER:5 5/10 cloud with certain large areas
covered, 4,000-8,000 feet. Visibility above clouds
unlimited, below clouds, 5-10 miles
TYPE OF ENEMY AIRCRAFT ENCOUNTERED:FW 190
CLAIM:Two FW 190s destroyed, one FW 190 damaged
```

After the squadron made its bombing run, we wandered southwest in the quest of enemy road and rail activities or to engage any enemy aircraft that could be found. As we flew over Mantes-Gassicourt, France, I looked down from 10,000 feet and thought I saw a truck convoy on the road just north of the Seine River. I led the squadron across the river and did a 180-degree turn to return. In the meantime, I ordered the lower six of my aircraft of my immediate support to follow me down to investigate the convoy. Lieutenant Rankin was told to circle aloft at 14,000 feet and give us cover.

The convoy proved to be piles of brown stones piled along the road, so we pulled up and climbed back up through a cloud level just above. Just as we broke out of the top of the cloud level, Lieutenant Rankin, in the top cover, reported three enemy aircraft climbing rapidly above the cloud level. He then said that many bandits were coming up.

We were hit by approximately 15 Me 109s and FW 190s. Everyone was breaking into them as fast as possible. I shot at two FW 190s above with considerable deflection, more to make them break than to hit them. Then, I immediately wheeled to the left to get out of the fire of an Me 109 that was firing to beat hell. He passed behind me from his 90-degree side approach and continued straight away, never waiting to turn back or recover. Six aircraft were immediately picked up two or three miles to the west and above. So, I continued to hold everything forward and climb in their direction. My difference in altitude and the distance that separated us caused me to lose some distance but gain some altitude. Somewhere past Evreux airdrome, I could only see two some 10 miles ahead of me. Those two did an abrupt turn to the southeast and started to fly toward Paris. Again, I picked up all six of them. The four leading were 5 miles ahead. At a point over Dreux airdrome, I bounced the two stragglers from 22,000 feet, only to discover that they were two of my own outfit who were chasing the Hun. I gave them orders to join up with me, as I was by myself, and we would pursue the four ahead. The two misinterpreted, probably due to the shortage of gas, and turned and went home.

The enemy, who were only specks toward Paris by now, were slowly climbing. I thought, "Here's a beautiful chance for a sneak kill." Again, the throttle was boosted and I pointed the ship upward. South of Paris, the four FW 190s did a right turn to head west, enabling me to cut off considerable distance. My altitude was about 27,000 feet, while theirs was approximately 20,000 feet. Again, somewhere over Chartres, France, they conveniently did a 180-degree turn and headed east. This last turn put me almost directly over them and the attack began. All flew in a company front as we do. As I drew to a point approximately 2,000 yards in the rear of the four, the leader did a 45-degree turn to the southeast, and everyone began to cross over. I picked out the last FW 190 and opened up with a 20-degree deflection shot. I hit him squarely after about 50 rounds. He went spinning off in flame, straight for the earth.

The remaining three completed the turn and flew a three-airplane company front. The element leader was picked out next, with me flying about 300 to 400 yards to the rear. I opened up on him directly astern, flying straight and level. It is definitely recalled that he rocked his wings and I rocked mine in return. He probably though I was his wingman, who I had just shot down in the crossover turn. He was saying over the R/T, "Hans, you bastard, move up in line abreast and stop flying in back of me." At any rate, I fired and fired at this pilot to finally tag him with a decent concentration, and he nosed over to go straight down.

The remaining two FWs were still flying line abreast and unconcerned. So I slid over behind the flight leader and opened fire. My tracers showed just as I hit him, and the jig was up. He immediately began kicking rudder to roll over on his back, and I swung over on the last man to shoot at him as he went down. No hits were seen. I claim a damage to the flight leader. Both were seen running like mad in a steep dive, so I climbed up to 29,000 feet and came screaming home. The combat was at 22,000–24,000 feet. I claim two FW 190s destroyed and one FW 190 damaged.

–Col. Hubert Zemke

GLOSSARY

A/C: Aircraft

A/D: Airdrome

API Ammunition: Armor-piercing incendiary

Bounce: To attack the enemy aircraft

B.S.T.: British Standard Time

CAVU: Ceiling and visibility unlimited

Chandrelles: A maneuver consisting of a high-speed, climbing reversal

Deflection, Deflection Shot: The act of shooting in front of an enemy aircraft so that his fighter flies into the bullets

E/A: Enemy aircraft

Fowler Flaps: a split type of aircraft flaps

Inches: A measurement of the amount of boost (and thus, extra power) produced by a forced-induction mechanism on an aircraft engine

I.P.: The point at which a bomb run was begun

Immelmann: An aerial reversal at the top of a loop

Lazy Eights: An aircraft maneuver consisting of lazy circles

Lead Box: A defensive formation of bombers

Lufbery: A defensive circle flown by a number of aircraft

M.E.W.: Microwave early warning stations set up in the Netherlands in November, 1944 used a radar technique to vector Allied fighter aircraft onto German formations

R/T: Radio transmitter

S/E: Single-engine aircraft

Split-ess: A maneuver in which the pilot inverts his aircraft and dives.

T/E: Twin-engine aircraft

U/I: Unidentified

Water Injection: A spray of water injected within an aircraft engine to provide emergency power

Windmilling: A state when an aircraft's engine turns although the engine is stopped

INDEX